SOLUTION-FOCUSED BRIEF THERAPY IN SCHOOLS

OXFORD WORKSHOP SERIES:

SCHOOL SOCIAL WORK ASSOCIATION OF AMERICA

Series Advisory Board

SOLUTION-FOCUSED BRIEF THERAPY IN SCHOOLS

A 360-Degree View of the Research and Practice Principles

SECOND EDITION

Johnny S. Kim, Michael S. Kelly, & Cynthia Franklin

OXFORD WORKSHOP SERIES

OXFORD
UNIVERSITY PRESS

OXFORD
UNIVERSITY PRESS

Oxford University Press is a department of the University of Oxford. It furthers the University's objective of excellence in research, scholarship, and education by publishing worldwide. Oxford is a registered trade mark of Oxford University Press in the UK and certain other countries.

Published in the United States of America by Oxford University Press
198 Madison Avenue, New York, NY 10016, United States of America.

First Edition published in 2008
Second Edition published in 2017

CIP data is on file at the Library of Congress
ISBN 978–0–19–060725–8

1 3 5 7 9 8 6 4 2

Printed by Webcom Inc., Canada

We dedicate this book to the pioneers of school social work, who started this profession in the early 20th century as a solution to the challenge of building school/home/community linkages; to the 30-plus national and state associations that carry on this work today; and to our school social work students, who are eager to become the next generation of strengths-based school social work practitioners.

Contents

Contributing Authors   *ix*

Chapter 1   Introduction: A 360-Degree View
of Solution-Focused Brief Therapy
in Schools   *1*
(Johnny S. Kim, Michael S. Kelly, & Cynthia Franklin)

Chapter 2   SFBT Techniques and Solution
Building   *12*
(Johnny S. Kim, Michael S. Kelly, & Cynthia Franklin)

Chapter 3   SFBT and Evidence-Based Practice: The
State of the Science   *31*
(Johnny S. Kim, Michael S. Kelly, & Cynthia Franklin)

Chapter 4   SFBT Within the Tier 1 Framework:
Alternative Schools Adopting the SFBT
Model   *52*
(Cynthia Franklin & Samantha Guz)

Chapter 5   SFBT Within the Tier 2 Framework:
Coaching Teachers to See the Solutions
in Their Classrooms   *74*
(Michael S. Kelly, Johnny S. Kim, & Cynthia Franklin)

Chapter 6   SFBT Within the Tier 3 Framework:
Case Examples of School Social Workers
Using SFBT   *87*
(Michael S. Kelly, Johnny S. Kim, & Cynthia Franklin)

Chapter 7   **SFBT in Action: Child Abuse and Neglect**   *107*
                   (Robert Blundo & Kristin W. Bolton)

Chapter 8   **SFBT in Action: Mental Health and Suicidal
                   Ideation**   *126*
                   (Carol Buchholz Holland)

Chapter 9   **SFBT in Action: Substance Use**   *153*
                   (Adam S. Froerer & Elliott E. Connie)

Chapter 10   **SFBT in Action: Eating Disorders**   *179*
                   (Karrie Slavin & Johnny S. Kim)

                   Index   *197*

Contributing Authors

Chapter 4: SFBT Within the Tier 1 Framework: Alternative Schools Adopting the SFBT Model
Samantha Guz, BS
School of Social Work
The University of Texas at Austin

Chapter 7: SFBT in Action: Child Abuse and Neglect
Robert Blundo, PhD
Kristin W. Bolton, PhD
Strengths/Solution-Focused Collaborative
School of Social Work
College of Health and Human Services
University of North Carolina–Wilmington

Chapter 8: SFBT in Action: Mental Health and Suicidal Ideation
Carol Buchholz Holland, PhD
Counselor Education Program
North Dakota State University

Chapter 9: SFBT in Action: Substance Use
Adam Froerer, PhD
The Connie Institute &
Mercer University School of Medicine

Elliott Connie, MA, LPC
The Connie Institute

Chapter 10: SFBT in Action: Eating Disorders
Karrie Slavins, MSW, MPH, LMSW
School of Social Work
Western Michigan &
Private Practice
Grand Rapids, Michigan

SOLUTION-FOCUSED BRIEF THERAPY IN SCHOOLS

1

■ ■ ■

Introduction

A 360-Degree View of Solution-Focused Brief Therapy in Schools

Johnny S. Kim, Michael S. Kelly, & Cynthia Franklin

Since its creation in the 1980s, solution-focused brief therapy (SFBT) has gradually become a common treatment option accepted by many mental health professionals (MacDonald, 2007). With its emphasis on client strengths and short-term treatment, SFBT appears to be well suited for school mental health contexts given the wide array of problems presenting in school settings and the large caseloads of most school social workers (Franklin, Biever, Moore, Clemons, & Scamardo, 2001; Newsome, 2005). This second edition is part of the Oxford Workshop Series and presents a "360-degree" view of SFBT in school settings from meta-analytic, intervention research, and practice perspectives.

All the chapters from the previous edition have been updated, and we have added new chapters to further expand the clinical examples demonstrating SFBT techniques. Since publication of the first edition in 2006, research on SFBT in schools has produced several advances that we cover here, including updates on recent systematic reviews and discussion about SFBT listed on national evidence-based registries. This second edition also expands some of the original chapters by adding a Response to Intervention (RtI) framework for schools that may want to use the SFBT approach. And we have added several new clinical chapters called "SFBT in Action." Selected based on results from the Second National School Social Work Survey, which identified the most common school-related problems that school social workers encounter in their work, these new clinical chapters further demonstrate ways to use SFBT with students.

The chapters in this book take you through a 360-degree view of SFBT in school social work practice. You will first learn about SFBT itself, from its earliest beginnings in the 1980s to the present day. In Chapter 2, SFBT techniques and why this approach can be applied directly to school social work practice realities are discussed. Additionally, the SFBT theory of change is presented to help explain how these techniques positively affect students. In Chapter 3, the question "Does SFBT really work?" is given a thorough review, including the most recent results from several systematic reviews and meta-analyses on SFBT practice and giving a full picture of the current state of the science in regards to SFBT practice. Chapter 4 provides a brief overview of Tier 1 goals and how SFBT can work within this RtI framework that is popular in schools. Chapter 4 focuses on one such school—Gonzalo Garza Independence High School in Austin, Texas—that the authors have consulted with extensively and that illustrates a solution-focused Tier 1 approach adopting SFBT ideas and principles throughout the entire school curriculum and discipline process. Chapter 5 discusses Tier 2 goals and how SFBT can be applied to targeted groups of students who are identified as more at-risk. It also features a particularly exciting new approach to using SFBT in schools—the WOWW program ("Working on What Works")—to illustrate how SFBT can be adapted to classroom and small group contexts. WOWW is a teacher coaching intervention designed to increase teacher-student collaboration for better learning environments, and along with a detailed description of the WOWW intervention program in the Chicago area (2007–2012), the promising outcome data from the initial WOWW program are analyzed and discussed. Chapter 6 draws on some of the positive outcomes of the Garza experience to show how school social workers in a diverse array of K-12 school environments have translated SFBT ideas using a Tier 3 approach (intensive individual counseling). And with Chapters 7 through 10 (the "SFBT in Action" chapters), this second edition expands on the practice by identifying four of the most common student problems encountered by school social workers and describing how to apply SFBT techniques to your school practice.

In Schools, Solutions Are Everywhere

Problems abound in school settings. Students are not always ready to learn, teachers are not always sure how to deal with the underachieving and/or defiant student and instead claim that he or she just "doesn't care," and parents are at times eager to find someone from the school to blame. The overall school climate provides additional possible stresses, with school violence, bullying, gang activity, and other illicit behavior happening on school grounds while school administrators try to maintain "zero tolerance" for these behaviors on the one hand yet foster a positive, child-centered learning environment to increase academic achievement for all students on the other. And as if all these problems were not enough, the field of education is under pressure from federal, state, and local governments to provide accurate and measurable progress toward yearly goals, a process that has become even more pronounced since implementation of the No Child Left Behind legislation in 2002.

Solutions, however, also abound in school settings. Second graders wake up early and tell their parents that they cannot wait to get to school so they can see their teachers and their friends. Teachers stop in the hallway to tell colleagues about a new project they are excited about starting with their students. In cafes, beauty shops, and church basements, parents encourage other parents to send their own kids to a child's school because of all the great things that school has going for it. School leaders, in collaboration with local law enforcement, parents, and the students themselves, create zones of safety even for children living in economically distressed and dangerous neighborhoods. All the school stakeholders (teachers, parents, kids, and administrators) welcome higher accountability standards and frame them as an opportunity to foster a more collaborative and high-achieving academic culture.

Schools can be places of solutions, strengths, and successes. School-based mental health professionals (school social workers, school counselors, and school psychologists) have numerous ways to harness the solutions that are already happening in their schools. A database search revealed more than 50 books in print on SFBT, SFBT associations in over 10 countries, and several annual national and international conferences devoted to SFBT. In Chapter 3, we share findings from a meta-analysis of SFBT studies that show solid (though modest) impacts in the current SFBT practice literature. Compared to a more heavily researched approach such as cognitive-behavioral therapy (CBT), SFBT is still developing rigorous outcome studies that demonstrate its effectiveness, but as Chapter 3 shows, this approach is on its way to joining CBT as a practice that has shown some empirical efficacy (Franklin, Trepper, Gingerich, & McCollum, 2012).

We are sharing a 360-degree view of an approach that is still a work in progress and to which additional empirical research, theory, and practical applications are being added each year. In the spirit of evidence-based practice transparency, we do not overstate or play down the available research on SFBT's effectiveness: we share these findings with you and let you join us in assessing how well these findings apply to your own practice style and school context.

Why SFBT Is Well Suited to School Social Work Practice

Problems and solutions, to the thinking of an SFBT school social worker, are always "abounding" in any school context. Indeed, one of the more liberating notions of SFBT is that change is continually happening, which requires our attention to be focused on the small changes that are making potentially large differences in the lives of our clients. What we do with those small, sometimes hard-to-see changes is what make us SFBT school social workers, and it could even make our school contexts become more solution focused in their approaches to the key educational issues of today.

The following short case example demonstrates how the possibilities for change are indeed "everywhere" and how skilled SFBT school social workers can harness change to help clients make big changes in their everyday school behavior. Read the example not only to know about the specific SFBT techniques in action (more on those later), but also to understand how the different members of the client system perceive the intervention being conducted by the solution-focused school social worker and then collaborate with the social worker to help students succeed.

> Bonita was one of the first students I met at my first-ever school social work position. She was lost, literally. She had just come to the school as a sixth grader and wasn't sure where her self-contained special education class was. She asked me for directions, and I introduced her to her teacher. The next week, she was in my office, crying about how much she missed her old school and didn't like the older kids at our junior high. She had announced to her teacher, "I hate this school, and I'm staying

at home tomorrow!" While I validated her feelings of sadness and anxiety, I asked if she had noticed anything getting better for her at our school. She said that she still had a good friend from her old school with her, and that they were in the same class together. I asked how she would rank her experience at our school so far on a scale of 1 to 10, with 10 being the highest on the scale. She asked through her tears, "Can you go lower than 1?!" I said, "Sure," and she said, "It's a 0."

I asked what would it take for her to say that being at our school deserved a score of 2 or 3, and she said, "A total miracle." I then asked her to imagine that just such a miracle had happened that night and to picture the next day, when she was at our school and everything was better for her here. In such a case, what would be the first thing she'd notice that was different? Bonita thought for a while and replied, "I would be able to open my locker by myself."

It turned out that Bonita had never used a combination lock before, and this had made her feel very anxious as well as inadequate because all the other kids in her class were already doing it without problems. We set a goal of working on her locker combination skills with her teacher, and within weeks, Bonita was smiling and laughing each morning as I watched her walk into school.

Like Bonita, schools themselves are going through their own transition in relation to the utilization of mental health services. Some policy makers and educational leaders call for schools to become "full-service operations," giving students and parents the mental health, vocational, and English-language training that external community agencies are not adequately providing. Still others claim that school-based mental health is an "extra" service and supportable only to the degree that it produces demonstrable differences in student academic achievement and thus allows students to compete successfully in the global economy. One of our colleagues remembers being told by a local superintendent that he would support our colleague's SFBT research project only if it made a measurable positive impact on "bottom-line" education issues for his K-8 district (in his case, this meant higher GPAs and increased attendance).

School leaders and parents are right in wanting more from school-based mental health services, and the profession itself has only begun to recognize the need for more transparency with community stakeholders about the relative effectiveness of the interventions we typically employ in our school practices. This book will equip you with a solid working knowledge of the ideas and techniques behind SFBT, acquaint you with the most current evidence on the overall effectiveness of SFBT, and finally, demonstrate several examples of school social workers making SFBT happen in their particular school contexts. It is our hope that by looking at SFBT from a 360-degree perspective, you will be ready to bring more specific SFBT ideas and techniques into your school in the coming years.

Advantages of SFBT in a School Setting

Why does this approach help in a school setting? Students, teachers, and parents are going to be visible to the school social worker even when they are not being "treated." In addition to using actual SFBT techniques to access strengths in students, school social workers have a unique opportunity to observe their students handling a variety of other challenges in their day-to-day contact with the school population (Box 1.1).

SFBT Is Strengths Based

The SFBT approach posits that people have strengths; moreover, SFBT says that those strengths are active, *right now*, in helping clients manage their situation. The issue is not that clients cannot solve their problem without additional training or somehow submitting to the school social workers' view of the problem. Rather, their own inherent strengths will ultimately be what they use to resolve their problem.

Box 1.1 Advantages of SFBT

- SFBT is strengths based
- SFBT is client centered
- SFBT makes small changes matter
- SFBT is portable
- SFBT is adaptable
- SFBT can be as brief (or as long) as you want it to be
- SFBT enables practitioners to gain cultural competence
- SFBT can be adapted to special education IEP goals

By not presuming that all clients are inherently in need of some treatment for a particular pathology or dysfunction, strengths-based school social workers are free to see their clients do a variety of things well and to ask questions that help their clients mobilize those inherent strengths to do something about the particular problems they face. In addition, school social workers usually have to document their work with clients by writing reports and case summaries: SFBT gives them ample opportunities not only to focus on their client's strengths but also to incorporate those strengths into their written assessments and other paperwork.

SFBT Is Client Centered

SFBT starts from where the client is at—and sometimes in dramatic and powerful ways, creating contexts in which clients can determine their own goals and decide how and where they wish to make changes in their lives. In school settings, a solution-oriented school social worker may be more likely to notice and respond to what clients, whether students or teachers, are actually asking for and wishing to change. In addition to increasing the likelihood that the clients will implement a particular intervention and maintain progress toward their goals, focusing on what the clients want to change also helps to make the whole referral and placement process in school settings more client focused and thus (hopefully) more effective than standard behavior modification plans, which might not always include the specific goals and wishes of every part of the client system.

SFBT Makes Small Changes Matter

One of the biggest challenges in school social work practice is the common complaint by parents, administrators, and teachers that change brought about for a particular student's emotional/behavioral problems is too slow or too "small." SFBT stands this thinking on its head and asks school social workers to focus on helping clients make small changes and then maintain these changes, the theory being that with those small successes in hand, clients will begin to see themselves as more capable of making larger changes in their lives. Again and again, we have seen this principle play out with students in our school social work practice: by making one part of a problem go away, or by helping teachers see one strength of a student who they had "given up on," larger changes became possible, and the clients went ahead and made those changes with minimal coaching or encouragement on our part.

SFBT Is Portable

Though SFBT started as and remains a set of techniques rooted in clinical psychotherapy, it can make a difference in numerous other nonclinical school settings. Almost anywhere in a school is a potential site for applying SFBT techniques or ideas: the class meeting where students scale their own behavior and then talk about what they would have to do differently for them to rate themselves higher the next week; the special education staffing conference where parents and teachers describe exceptions when a student does not display a problem behavior in an effort to discover what the learning environment (and student) might do differently to avoid repeating the problem behavior; the playground mediation where students think about how doing one thing differently might change a conflict they are having. All these examples (and many more that you will read about in this book) underline the various ways that school social workers can bring SFBT into their diverse settings and adapt SFBT ideas to their multiple roles within their schools.

SFBT Is Adaptable

SFBT can be folded or nested into other techniques being used by clinicians. Most experienced school social workers we have worked with have characterized their practice approach as "eclectic." One of the best features of SFBT as a maturing practice approach is its ability to be integrated into other such approaches. Clearly, elements of SFBT fit nicely within a cognitive or behavioral treatment framework. Even practitioners who tend to favor approaches that are based more on discovering how the past impacts a student's current functioning will appreciate the aspects of SFBT where clients set goals for their own progress and gauge how well they are doing based on scaling questions.

SFBT Can Be as Brief (Or as Long) as You Want It to Be

One of the frequent complaints we hear about SFBT is that it is too surface oriented and too brief to get into the "real work." This may have been a fair criticism of SFBT in its early stages (when the approach was deliberately defined as being opposed to long-term treatment), but now, SFBT is clearly and easily adapted to single-session, brief, and long-term treatment processes. The nature of SFBT (the thinking that change is possible and constant) does not mean that clients who have more long-term treatment plans, such as those students in schools who have individualized education plans (IEPs) requiring a year of social work services, cannot benefit from the strengths-based approach inherent to SFBT. In our practice experience, some students we saw on a long-term basis wound up having several distinct SFBTs over the course of the year. The process of helping them was similar, but the issues changed as students learned how to manage one problem and then faced a new one.

SFBT Enables Practitioners to Gain Cultural Competence

All school personnel (school social workers included) are realizing the increasing importance of cultural competence skills in helping them to engage with and teach students from diverse backgrounds. Several recent scholars have noted that one of the main persisting aspects of the racial "achievement gap" is the cultural competence gap that separates white educators from the students of color whom they are trying to empower and teach (Delpit & Kohl, 2006; Ferguson, 2002; Tripod Project, 2007). By emphasizing how clients perceive their problems and how they might devise solutions that fit their own preferences, SFBT appears well suited to help school social workers practice from an approach of cultural humility. In addition, through the example of SFBT pioneers like Insoo Kim Berg, SFBT has always advocated that clinicians frequently adopt "one-down" positions that allow clients to be in charge of their treatment in ways that avoid clients perceiving the school social worker as pushy or domineering. Clinicians who are perceived as authoritarian or interested only in their own particular approach to treatment are often labeled as culturally insensitive by minorities who are receiving mental health treatment (Fong, 2004; McGoldrick, Giordano, & Pearse, 1996; Wing Sue & McGoldrick, 2005), and SFBT clearly offers an alternate way for school social workers to engage clients in clinical work without making them feel forced to adopt the social workers' worldview. Furthering this idea of cultural humility in the SFBT approach, Kim (2014) describes ways to use SFBT techniques and questions from a multicultural perspective with clients.

SFBT Can Be Adapted to Special Education IEP Goals

For many school social workers, a lot of their services are delivered to students who have yearly goals for treatment, usually expressed through an

---

IEP. SFBT, along with CBT, is well suited to helping school social workers write those goals and collaborate with their clients to meet those goals successfully. By identifying discrete changes and applying scaling questions, school social workers can easily integrate SFBT thinking into their IEP goals. So far, this area has not been studied empirically, but our contention, from our own school experience, is that the very process of creating IEP goals with students, teachers, and parents in a solution-focused manner enhanced the eventual achievement of those goals by motivating the client system to move toward solutions rather than remain stuck at only talking about the problem.

Summary

SFBT is well suited to school social work practice and school contexts. A solution-focused school social worker can help students, particularly those who are harder to reach, focus on what's working and how they can change their lives in positive ways. Although not originally created for application in a school context, SFBT is clearly an adaptable, portable practice philosophy that, as we will see, can be used in many diverse school contexts at multiple levels of intervention.

References

Delpit, L., & Kohl, H. (2006). *Other people's children: Cultural conflict in the classroom* (2nd ed.). New York: New Press.

Ferguson, R. (October 21, 2002). What doesn't meet the eye: Understanding and addressing racial disparities in high-achieving suburban schools from The Tripod Project Background. Retrieved August 1, 2007, from http://www.tripodproject.org/uploads/file/What_doesnt_meet_the_eye.pdf

Fong, R. (2004). Immigrant and refugee children and families. In R. Fong (Ed.), *Culturally competent social work practice with immigrant children and families*. New York: Guilford Press.

Franklin, C., Biever, J., Moore, K., Clemons, D., & Scamardo, M. (2001). The effectiveness of solution-focused therapy with children in a school setting. *Research on Social Work Practice, 11*(4), 411–434.

Franklin, C., Trepper, T., Gingerich, W., & McCollum, E. (2012). *Solution-focused brief therapy: A handbook of evidence-based practice*. New York: Oxford University Press.

Kim, J. S. (2014). *Solution-focused brief therapy: A multicultural approach*. Thousand Oaks: CA: Sage Publications.

MacDonald, A. J. (2007). *Solution-focused therapy: Theory, research and practice*. London: Sage Books.

McGoldrick, M., Giordano, J., & Pearse, J. K. (1996). *Ethnicity and family therapy* (2nd ed.). New York: Guilford Press.

Newsome, S. (2005). The impact of solution-focused brief therapy with at-risk junior high school students. *Children & Schools, 27*(2), 83–90.

Tripod Project. (2007). Background of Tripod research project. Retrieved August 1, 2007, from http://www.tripodproject.org/index.php/about/about_background/

Wing Sue, D., & McGoldrick, M. (2005). *Multicultural social work practice.* New York: Wiley.

2

■ ■ ■

SFBT Techniques and Solution Building

Johnny S. Kim, Michael S. Kelly, & Cynthia Franklin

The History

In the late 1970s, psychotherapy in the United States was at its zenith. The evidence for this high point was everywhere: mental health services had gone mainstream, self-help books topped the best-seller lists, and perhaps most important, economic conditions had created a high degree of health insurance support for mental health services (Cushman, 1995; Moskowitz, 2001; Wylie, 1994). The insurance money for psychotherapy usually was not time limited and was also generous, allowing therapists from psychiatry, psychology, and social work to earn six-figure incomes. A review of the popular and academic literature of that time reveals that three main schools of psychotherapy were popular then: psychodynamic therapy, cognitive-behavioral therapy (CBT), and humanistic psychology (Norcross & Goldried, 2003). Therapy was available, usually open ended or long term, to almost anyone who knew where to find it.

By the early 1990s, things had changed dramatically. Self-help books continued to crowd American bookstore shelves, but psychotherapy had become a profession that was largely dominated by managed care. Although still readily available to many people who needed it, psychotherapy was now time limited, often restricted to no more than 20 sessions a year. Fees for therapists had been capped as well, and the golden days of lucrative therapy practices had begun to fade (Duncan, Hubble, & Miller, 1999; Lipchik, 1994; Wylie, 1994). To a psychoanalytically informed practitioner used to seeing patients for a decade or more, this new era was dreary indeed.

Something else important happened in psychotherapy during this era, however, and in the heart of America, in a city known more for bratwurst and beer than for therapeutic innovation. In Milwaukee, Wisconsin, a group of therapists led by Insoo Kim Berg and Steve de Shazer started working with clients in radically different ways. They only saw clients for a few sessions, often no more than five or six times. They asked questions that focused less on client problems and more on how clients had previously solved the problems they faced. The focus was on using solutions from the past to handle issues of the present and future. Although consciousness of a client's experience of loss, trauma, and other difficult feelings was incorporated into their work, these therapists were more focused on the client's actual strengths and capacities to move beyond those difficult issues quickly (Berg, 1994; de Shazer, 1988). The SFBT model for working with clients required a different mind-set and a unique line of questioning compared to the more popular CBT approach.

In SFBT, clients themselves are viewed as experts on their own problems and solutions. Rather than position therapists as authority figures or experts in the counseling sessions, this new approach put therapists in the role of curious questioners who also offer suggestions that both bring out client strengths and set them on the path to finding their own solution, not the answer or solution that the school social worker had chosen for the client. Overall, the presumption of the therapists in Milwaukee was that clients could change, would change, and were actually changing already. These therapists were creating a new approach to therapy, a collection of techniques and activities that would eventually become known as SFBT (Berg, 1994; De Jong & Berg, 2002; de Shazer, 1988; MacDonald, 2007). Box 2.1 shows some differences between SFBT and CBT treatment.

SFBT Theory of Change

While learning about the different SFBT techniques are important for school social workers, understanding how those techniques work to create changes in students can be very useful in grasping the SFBT mentality and approach. Positive emotions were noted early in the development of SFBT. For example, de Shazer (1985) discussed the importance of increasing positive expectancy (i.e., hope) and suggested the perception that change is possible is a critical part of the SFBT processes that help clients change. Insoo Kim Berg also frequently discussed the importance of fostering hope in clients and

Box 2.1 Difference Between SFBT and CBT

SFBT SOCIAL WORKER MODEL

- What could be a small step toward achieving your goal?
- What has been going well in your life?
- What will you be doing differently when the problem is no longer present?
- How did you know that was the right thing to do?

CBT SOCIAL WORKER MODEL

- How does it make you feel when the problem occurs?
- When does the problem occur in your life?
- What thoughts do you have when the problem occurs?
- How do others react when you are behaving that way?

described how solution-focused conversations create a sense of competence, which is also important for helping clients change (e.g., Berg & Dolan, 2001; De Jong & Berg, 2008). Despite such efforts to understand the therapeutic process of SFBT, our knowledge about the possible theoretical and therapeutic mechanisms for change within SFBT are still in their infancy when it comes to actual empirical studies that examine these mechanisms, especially concerning the role that positive emotions may play in the change process of SFBT.

With the recent popularity of positive psychology and research on positive emotions such as hope, an opportunity exists to re-examine how SFBT techniques work in the counseling sessions. Positive emotions theory argues that positive emotions are not simply the absence of negative emotions (e.g., anger, sad, frustrated, and hopelessness) or just a "good feeling" the student has but, rather, can serve as a therapeutic value in clinical practice (Fitzpatrick & Stalikas, 2008a). Most of the research and discussion in clinical practice has viewed positive emotions as a desired outcome (i.e., "I want to be happy again") and neglected the possibility of positive emotions serving as a vehicle for change (Fitzpatrick & Stalikas, 2008b). We believe that the broaden-and-build theory of positive emotions by Fredrickson (1998) may provide some the most compelling evidence for explaining how SFBT works and may be used in future research studies to examine change processes within SFBT.

Under the broaden-and-build theory, positive emotions further elicit thought-action repertoires that are broad, flexible, and receptive to new thoughts and actions, whereas negative emotions elicit thought-action repertoires that are limited, rigid, and less receptive. The broadening aspect of this theory posits that after someone experiences a positive feeling, that person is more open and more receptive. This may be the key step in helping students observe exceptions, make new meanings, and *do something different* that is touted in SFBT practice literature (de Shazer, 1991). In addition to broadening, this theory also posits that positive emotions help build durable resources that can be drawn upon for future use. Students experiencing psychological problems like depression or anxiety commonly to dwell on negative thoughts and beliefs about themselves or a particular situation, which then leads to dysfunctional behaviors and further perpetuates a downward spiral of psychopathology (Garland, Fredrickson, Kring, Johnson, Meyer, & Penn, 2010). With positive emotions, the opposite can occur: upward spirals of positive emotions help students build enduring resources of new thoughts, perspectives, and options (Fitzpatrick & Stalikas, 2008b). But to counteract the negative emotions students experience, a greater number of positive emotions must be experienced. Research suggests that, at minimum, a 3-to-1 ratio of positive emotions experienced to negative emotions is necessary to help generate sustained positive changes and undo the impact of negative distress (Garland et al., 2010). Therapeutic techniques for increasing positive emotion are fairly new to positive psychology and are still being developed. However, techniques for increasing client strengths and positive emotions are not new to SFBT; they have existed for many years and have been successfully applied in diverse practice settings (Kim & Franklin, 2015). Formulating answers to solution-focused questions requires students to think about their relationships and talk about their experiences in different ways, turning their problem perceptions and negative emotions into positive formulations for change.

The Skills

As the Solution-Focused Brief Therapy Association (SFBTA) makes clear, "[SFBT] should be characterized as a way of clinical thinking and interacting with clients more than a list of techniques" (SFBTA, 2006, p. 2). By viewing a client as being engaged in a constant process of change, solution-focused clinicians are poised to tap into that client's natural ways of healing and existing ways of viewing change (Tallman & Bohart, 1999). In July 2013, the second edition of the *Solution Focused Therapy Treatment Manual for Working with Individuals* was published on the SFBTA website for clinicians to learn more about the clinical practices and research relevant to SFBT. It is free to download at www.sfbta.org and a great resource for learning more SFBT techniques.

How SFBT Distinguishes Itself

Rather than a set of sequential techniques that must be followed rigidly, SFBT is more of an approach (SFBTA, 2006). Every client is different, and every professional using SFBT is going to adapt his or her approach to the specific client's needs and developmental level. This is perhaps most evident in a school setting, where the client's age can range from 5 years (a kindergartner) to 65 years (a veteran principal). We focus here on how, in the first session, SFBT distinguishes itself from other treatment models by providing some examples of not only how to "start" doing SFBT but also how to contextualize the different directions SFBT can take depending on the client's goals and frame of reference.

An emphasis of SFBT is on the process of developing a future solution rather than analyzing and dissecting the past manifestation of the problem. SFBT practitioners focus on identifying past successes and exceptions to the problem, as well as on identifying new and novel ways of responding in future efforts to solve problems (Franklin, Biever, Moore, Clemons, & Scamardo, 2001). Orchestrating a positive and solution-focused conversation, often referred to as *solution building*, is unique to SFBT and aims to create a context for change in which hope, competence, and positive expectancies increase and a client can co-construct with the therapist workable solutions to problems. The task of the school social worker is to listen for words and phrases that are aspects of a solution for the student and build on those (Berg & De Jong, 2008). There is a constant focus by the school social worker on not delving into problem talk but, rather, helping the student identify what life looks like when the problem is gone and what the student will be doing differently (Kim, 2014). This is one of the key differences between SFBT and other strengths-based interventions like motivational interviewing (MI). A recent microanalysis conducted by Korman, Bavelas, and De Jong (2013) found that SFBT counselors preserved the client's exact words at a significantly higher rate, while adding their own interpretations at a significantly lower rate, than MI and CBT counselors. This study also showed how a SFBT approach differs from other, similar approaches like MI by highlighting the sustained focus on listening for what the clients want, what's important to the clients, and how clients can achieve their desired version of themselves (Bavelas et al., 2013).

When school social workers meet with students, much of the counseling session is centered around questions or problem-solving discussions. Typically, the types of questions asked are:

- Questions about the student's problem
- Questions about mistakes made
- Questions about causes of the student's problem
- Questions about how the problems making the student feel

As these types of questions show, most approaches to counseling focus on the problem, with little talk about the solutions or what the student wants that is different from the current situation. This solution-building mindset differs from more problem-focused approaches like CBT that focus on helping clients identify problem thinking and beliefs, challenging those negative thinking patterns, and substituting more rational thoughts and beliefs. The solution-focused techniques described below help school social workers accomplish this task and stay focused on the SFBT approach.

Pre-session Change, Exception Questions, and Other Key SFBT Techniques

One distinctive facet of the SFBT approach is the attention that the solution-focused school social worker pays to changes that are already in motion from the moment the first session is scheduled. This is called *pre-session change*, and it allows the solution-focused school social worker to model the SFBT concept not only that change is a natural and constant occurrence, but also that this notion can become a source of hope and empowerment for clients as they struggle to change what initially seem to be overwhelming problems they fear will take years of treatment to address (Berg, 1994; De Jong & Berg, 2001; Murphy, 1996; Selekman, 2005). To do this, solution-focused school social workers at the first meeting ask questions such as "Since we last talked on the phone and scheduled this first meeting, what's been better in the way that you and your son are getting along at home?" or "Since Mrs. Smith asked me to come and see you, have there been any positive changes in the way you're behaving in her class?" On the basis of any changes that the client identifies, the solution-focused school professional moves on to amplify those positive changes and sees what ideas the student might have about maintaining such changes into the future. Box 2.2 describes questions typically used in SFBT.

Box 2.2 Typical Questions in SFBT

Coping Questions

- How do you keep from giving up since you have tried everything?
- How have you managed to cope so far?
- What keeps you hanging in there?
- What has been going well in your life?

Looking for Solutions

- What small change will you notice when things are different?
- How would you know if our talk make a big difference?
- What has been better for you this week?
- When didn't you have this problem? Even a little bit?

Relationship Questions

- What will your teacher notice about your behavior when things have changed?
- How would your parents know you were at your best? What would you be doing that lets them know?
- What would your teacher notice about you when things are better?

Moving Forward

- What will you do instead of cutting class to smoke?
- What will be a small sign that you are no longer depressed?
- What will you notice about yourself that is different? What will others notice about you that is different?
- How could you do more of that this week?

A hopeful, almost expectant tone pervades SFBT sessions, where students and parents are welcomed and given the chance to describe how they are already changing before they have even begun treatment. In our practice experience, we have seen this approach resonate with students used to mental health professionals who start their first sessions trying to probe for underlying causes to the problem behavior by asking detailed questions about the student's history. By setting the context squarely in the present and asking clients to imagine a new, preferred future, many students embrace this perspective and tailor it to their own goals. We have also found students are more willing to talk about things they do well or things they like compared to talking about their problems. This can be especially useful when students are hesitant about seeing a school social worker as well as helpful in quickly developing a therapeutic relationship. And it can be particularly important when working with students who are ethnic minorities as this allows the school social worker to practice cultural humility.

This approach is immediately apparent through the ways that solution-focused clinicians talk with their students from the first session. Solution-focused school social workers tend to focus on different areas in their initial contact with students compared to typical treatment approaches, which are more rooted in using the medical model to assess for student pathology. The questions tend to focus on what the students see as their presenting problem, and little time is spent talking about root causes or past family history that might have contributed to the problem. Rather, from the first meeting, students are encouraged to talk about their situation in present and future terms, with the expectation communicated that they are more in charge of their problem now than they might have previously felt. In contrast to a typical first session, in which great energy and effort is expended by both the school social worker and the student to describe the problem and all its attendant impacts for the student, solution-focused school social workers tend to ask students to tell them what they might have already tried to address the problem and, if that the student cannot name anything that has worked, identify those times or situations where the problem is not present (or at least not as problematic).

Students are also encouraged to think of their preferred future self, even in the first session. This can be done through questions that orient the session toward future hopes and what will be different when the problem is no longer there. More specifically, by asking students the "miracle question" or "scaling questions," they are invited to imagine a future reality that they might be able to start bringing into being. For the miracle question, students are asked to imagine that when they go to bed that night, a miracle takes place, and when they wake up, their problem is solved and they feel better and more hopeful about their day. The solution-focused school social worker then asks, "What would be the first thing you would notice about your new situation that told you the miracle had taken place?" This opens up the possibilities that students can see changes happening in their lives and identify first steps at achieving more of the changes they want (Berg, 1994). Scaling questions can be used for a variety of subjects, asking clients to rate their ability to manage their problem on a scale of 1 to 5, with 1 being "not able to handle my problem at all" and 5 being "fully able to handle my problem." Assuming a student rates the problem as being at a 2, a solution-focused school social worker can ask what the student would be doing differently if he or she is able to give a rating of 3 or 4 when they meet the next week. With the scales, students can be asked to imagine what they would need to do to raise (or lower, depending on the way the scale is framed) their score, and exceptions where they may have already been doing things more in line with their goals can be identified.

Likewise, the focus on exception questions helps the student use the past pragmatically. By identifying times when the problem was not affecting the student, or when the student was more able to handle a similar situation successfully, the solution-focused school social worker invites the student to view his or her current reality as being less stuck and hopeless. It also encourages the student to imagine that the "exceptions" could more easily become the future reality because, as one student told us, "Hey, now that I realize that it's already been a problem I was able to beat before, why can't I do it again?"

Future Sessions and Goal Setting

Like many treatment approaches, SFBT favors the implementation of a goal-setting process between student and school social worker. Where SFBT differs is in the power sharing that goes on when setting these goals. Instead of a process where, over time, students are expected to face their denial and accept a reality that the school social worker is advocating, the reality of the student is always paramount in the sessions. (This produces some interesting contrasts—and even conflicts—when working in school settings with children referred by teachers, which we discuss more fully in Chapter 5.)

Students can change as much or as little as they want, and they are given the freedom by the SFBT process to set goals they can achieve. In some ways, this goal-setting process mirrors some of what CBT school social workers do as they set treatment goals with clients based on specific problematic thinking or behavior. The difference between CBT and SFBT here is that students are not required to adopt a particular approach to their behavior or adopt new ways of thinking about how their emotions are affected by their cognitions. In CBT, the school social worker typically assigns tasks and makes recommendations for behavioral or thought changes, whereas an SFBT approach encourages students to do more of their own previous exception behaviors in an effort to achieve their preferred future self (Bavelas et al., 2013).

Compliments Count

Anyone watching a videotape of a clinician doing SFBT will be immediately struck by how often the clinician compliments the client over the course of a regular session (Berg, 1994). Because in SFBT so much effort is spent identifying student resiliency and setting goals based on strengths that students have demonstrated in the past, it's understandable that students begin to self-report the times between sessions that they have made at least small gains in solving their problems. Rather than take credit for helping the student make this change (or expressing frustration the student is not progressing more quickly), solution-focused school social workers are quick to highlight client gains and give compliments about their progress.

These compliments are not meant to be patronizing. Good solution-focused school social workers know how to convey genuine pride and excitement at a student's progress, often saying things like "That's great; tell me how you did that?" or "I am so impressed! What did you figure out that helped you deal with your problem so successfully?" Students take that feedback and are motivated to make more changes, either for the same problem or for a different problem that the solution-focused school social worker may not even be aware of yet (De Jong & Berg, 2002; Metcalf, 1995; Selekman, 2005).

Coping Questions

One persistent critique of SFBT has been that it is too optimistic and does not allow clients to have deep emotional experiences in therapy (Lipchik, 1994; Nylund & Corsiglia, 1994). This has been acknowledged as a critique by SFBT's founders (Miller & de Shazer, 2000), but in some ways, it strikes us as a straw-man argument. If clients have strong, upsetting emotional experiences in treatment, they are certainly encouraged by a solution-focused school social worker to experience those feelings—to cry, to yell, to express what they need to express. What SFBT does not do, and which confuses some people who are new to the approach, is place any inherent value on intense emotional experiences in therapy (Berg & Dolan, 2001; De Jong & Berg, 2001). Because SFBT presumes that students can (and regularly do) solve their own problems, no particular weight is given to any emotionally cathartic experience that might be triggered by the school social worker during sessions. Instead, great emphasis is placed on asking questions that allow students to help the school social worker learn what the students want to talk about, as well as how fast or slow the students would like to go in exploring how to change their situation. In our two decades of doing solution-focused work in schools, we have witnessed many students share their hopes and goals in SFBT with intense emotion; we have also seen many students embrace the approach in a calm, somewhat playful way, with plenty of laughter and spontaneity punctuating the sessions. The focus has never been on the degree of emotional intensity or on asking them how they feel about something; rather, it has always been on helping students generate their own solutions (Berg, 1994; Miller & de Shazer, 2000). In fact, recently focus on SFBT has been on how the approach creates positive emotions in students, which helps them change (discussed more in *SFBT Theory of Change* below).

The most concrete way to show how this approach works for chronic and seemingly debilitating problems that students deal with is the SFBT coping questions. Solution-focused school social workers often use these questions when a student is reporting significant difficulty and even some frustration that a situation has not gotten better. Questions like "This situation sounds really hard—how have you managed to cope with it as well as you have thus far?" are designed to elicit student strengths and possible strategies that they may have used in the past to cope with their difficulties (Berg, 1994; Selekman, 2005). Another coping question that we have often used when students are complaining about the seeming impossibility of their situations is "How have you been able to keep this from getting worse for you?" By framing the "impossible" situation as one that the student has some control over, the solution-focused school social worker can explore what hidden capacities the student has for managing and potentially overcoming problems.

Doing Something Different

One of the most exciting and fun aspects of doing SFBT in a school setting is the ability to try out new ideas and interventions with students based on their willingness to "do something different" about their problem. Rather than seek to teach students a specific technique for handling their problems, such as those associated with anger or difficulty in making friends, solution-focused school social workers explore what students have done about their problems in the past and what new ideas they could try now. For example, an 11-year-old student we worked with was struggling to manage his temper in the classroom and had not found the traditional cognitive-behavioral anger management techniques offered by his special education teacher to be helpful. He told us that he had run out of ideas because everything he had tried before had not worked. When we told him that we thought it might be time to "do something different," he immediately warmed up to the idea and started brainstorming new ideas to tackle his anger problem. Being a young person, some of the ideas were admittedly wacky: no teacher was likely to let him play games on his iPad all day to fend off his tirades, for example. After sifting through his ideas, however, the student settled on a creative solution that he was excited to implement and that we thought his teacher would support as well: he would work out with his teacher a list of "helper tasks" in the class that he would be able to do any time he thought he was going to lose his temper. The teacher would get some help with things in the classroom, and the student would get to take his mind off his frustration and recharge.

Client Resistance? We Do Not See It that Way . . .

The advantage of having concepts like coping questions, "doing something different," brainstorming, or exception questions when working with students is that they allow a solution-focused school social worker to quickly short-circuit student resistance to working on their problems. In fact, the very concept of resistance is eagerly debated in the SFBT literature (Berg, 1994; de Shazer, 1988; O'Hanlon & Bertolino, 1998); most SFBT writers consider resistance to be more a product of the solution-focused professional's inability to find common ground with the student than an actual refusal by students to face their problems directly. By approaching the student in a respectful, patient way, we have found that the ideas in SFBT allow us not only to find some workable goal for most students in a school setting but also to avoid labeling our students as being "in denial" about their problems.

What SFBT Does (and Does Not) Teach

Part of what has held back SFBT in some quarters is the notion that it does not "teach" anything new to a student. Perhaps predictably, SFBT practitioners often define this relative lack of specific skill training as another strength of the approach—namely, it does not limit interventions to specific techniques that are generated by the school social worker. For one thing, it's usually easier to get people to do things that they already know how to do (Berg, 1994; De Jong & Berg, 2002; Selekman, 2005). SFBT works hard to help students identify the strengths and skills they already possess to address their problems, and then tries to free them up to "do more of what's working" (Berg, 1994; Newsome, 2004).

Another challenge to applying SFBT in a school involves the belief of some educators that they are there to instruct students on how to "act." Some educators who feel this moral imperative may be uncomfortable with SFBT's view of starting from where students truly are, and then working with what's there, as opposed to modeling a better way to behave or think. As stated earlier, the benefit of SFBT is that it does not deny the presenting problems that require intervention (e.g., student defiance or work refusal). It just frames them differently than the traditional school practice that typically emphasizes the authority of the adult over the self-determination of the student.

Undoubtedly, some educators can (and do) view SFBT as excessively optimistic and too "easy" on kids. SFBT does impart to clients an optimistic and future-oriented perspective; however, we believe there is value in this approach. Again and again, we have seen in our school practices how SFBT can elicit new ideas from students who have traditionally viewed their problems from more fatalistic and pessimistic angles. This can involve teaching new ideas to students, so SFBT in no way limits the skill and authority of the teacher or school social worker using it to engage with and help a student. If anything, we have often noticed that the process of asking SFBT questions itself makes an impression on students who are unsure how to respond to treatment and are anxious about seeing a mental health professional. By starting with a curious and hopeful stance, SFBT tries to de-escalate many potentially difficult situations and move the focus to solving problems that the student is having.

Finally, as a wholly student-centered treatment approach, SFBT is open to almost any intervention that is already underway in a student's life and, in the student's view, is a helpful intervention. For example, one student of ours was already taking anti-anxiety medication when we first met her, and part of the solution-focused treatment we conducted was helping her identify ways to build on the benefits she was seeing from taking her medication. In this way, students and school social workers can collaborate on using SFBT with other treatment models (e.g., psychoeducation or psychopharmacology) that emphasize students setting goals and working toward them. As discussed in Chapter 1, the portability and adaptability of SFBT in a school setting is one of the major strengths we have seen when applying this approach for the past two decades.

The Application

The later "SFBT in Action" chapters provide more concrete case examples of how to use SFBT with five of the most common issues or problems school social workers encounter. In the present chapter, we also include an example of a solution-focused handout developed by Franklin and Streeter (2004) to help students set goals using SFBT techniques (see Box 2.3) and a form developed by Garner (2004) to help practitioners evaluate their school's readiness to adopt SFBT ideas (see Box 2.4).

The Research

In Chapter 3, we share more information about the effectiveness of SFBT in schools and other mental health settings obtained since the first edition of this book. In our work employing meta-analytic techniques to analyze the extant intervention studies on SFBT, we have found that this therapy has a small to medium treatment effects on behaviors and problems typically found in a school setting. This outcome is only slightly smaller than the typical effect of other psychotherapeutic treatments for some of the same behaviors and problems experienced by students (Kim, 2008).

As we note in the next chapter, in keeping with our efforts to be transparent and rigorous in this book, we can highlight the claims of SFBT's effectiveness but also caution against overstating that, as a technique, SFBT outperforms all other approaches to therapy. In some ways, SFBT may be best viewed as an important technique to use with students because it facilitates

Box 2.3 Measuring Your Success

NAME _____ DATE _____

What were your goals for the previous semester? Check the goals that were *fully* met.

When it comes to meeting your goals, what are the obstacles that get in your way?

Choose 1 of the obstacles you listed and design a plan to overcome it.

OBSTACLE	WHAT I CAN DO	RESOURCES THAT CAN HELP

Having reviewed your goals, measure your progress on a scale of 1 to 10, with 1 being no progress and 10 being goal met.

Scaling allows you to see your progress on a continuum. Consider the following criteria before marking the number that represents your progress:

- Attendance
- Number of assignments completed
- Quality of work done

Circle the number that represents your progress.

1   2   3   4   5   6   7   8   9   10

What are 3 goals that you will set for the next semester?

1.
2.
3.

Describe what it will look like, sound like, and feel like when you are meeting all of the goals you have set for yourself.

Source: Franklin and Streeter (2004).

Box 2.4 Planning Exercise for Developing Solution-Building Schools

Characteristics of a Solution-Building School

Rate your school on a scale of 1 to 10, with 1 being the characteristic is absent and 10 being the school truly represents the trait.

Faculty emphasis on building relationships with students

1   2   3   4   5   6   7   8   9   10

Attention given to individual strengths of students

1   2   3   4   5   6   7   8   9   10

Emphasis upon student choices and personal responsibility

1   2   3   4   5   6   7   8   9   10

Overall commitment to achievement and hard work

1   2   3   4   5   6   7   8   9   10

Trust in student self-evaluation

1   2   3   4   5   6   7   8   9   10

Focus on the student's future successes instead of past difficulties

1   2   3   4   5   6   7   8   9   10

Celebrating small steps toward success

1   2   3   4   5   6   7   8   9   10

Reliance on goal setting activities

1   2   3   4   5   6   7   8   9   10

Source: Garner (2004).

---

conversations about student strengths. whereas many other approaches in schools (with competing claims of effectiveness) are more rooted in medical/deficit models. What remains for further research to explore is whether strengths-based approaches like SFBT produce better outcomes for students than approaches rooted in special education deficit models or social skills/psychoeducation models.

The Future

School settings and SFBT are in some ways a natural fit. School social workers are constantly struggling with large caseloads and limited time to serve all the students who need help, and SFBT's emphasis on rapid engagement and change for students can help school-based professionals meet more students and make a difference for them quickly. The goal-setting process of SFBT (involving scaling questions and asking teachers to observe behaviors that students are working on improving) can be easily adapted to the outcome-based education paperwork of Medicaid and special education to help school social workers document their effectiveness (Lever, Anthony, Stephan, Moore, Harrison, & Weist, 2006).

The challenge of finding ways to bring a solution-focused perspective using student, family, and teacher strengths into a variety of school contexts (e.g., special education staffing, disciplinary meetings, or teacher consultations) is significant, however, and sometimes even daunting. This is particularly true as educators increasingly favor "problem-talk" using diagnostic categories derived from special education classification and psychopathology language found in the *Diagnostic and Statistical Manual of Mental Disorders* (Altshuler & Kopels, 2003; House, 2002). More research on SFBT in schools (as well as collaboration between SFBT researchers and practitioners in schools) remains essential to help continue the work that Insoo Kim Berg and Steve de Shazer envisioned three decades ago.

Summary

SFBT is an approach that started in the American Midwest and has now spread throughout the world, heavily influencing the last two generations of practitioners. Its main ideas—that client strengths matter, that client change is constant, and that clients can be trusted to devise solutions to their own problems—are a welcome alternative to many of the deficit-based diagnostic and treatment approaches prevalent in schools today. Solution-focused school social workers can use techniques like the miracle question, coping questions, and scaling questions to identify student goals and strengths to help them make changes in their lives.

References

Altshuler, S. J., & Kopels, S. (2003). Advocating in schools for children with disabilities: What's new with IDEA? *Social Work, 48*(3), 320–329.

Bavelas, J., De Jong, P., Franklin, C., Froerer, A., Gingerich, W., Kim, J., Korman, H., Langer, S., Lee, M. Y., McCollum, E. E., Smock Jordan, S., & Trepper, T. S. (2013, July 1). Solution-focused therapy treatment manual for working with individuals, 2nd version. Retrieved from http://www.sfbta.org/researchdownloads.html

Berg, I. K. (1994). *Family-based services*. New York: W. W. Norton.

Berg, I., & Dolan, Y. (2001). *Tales of solutions: A collection of hope-inspiring stories*. New York: W. W. Norton.

Cushman, P. (1995). *Constructing the self, constructing America: A cultural history of psychotherapy*. Reading, MA: Addison-Wesley.

De Jong, P., & Berg, I. (2001). *Instructor's resource manual of interviewing for solutions*. New York: Brooks/Cole.

De Jong, P., & Berg, I. (2002). *Interviewing for solutions* (2nd ed.). New York: Brooks/Cole.

De Jong, P., & Berg, I. (2008). *Interviewing for solutions* (3rd ed.) Belmont, CA: Brooks/Cole-Thomson Learning.

de Shazer, S. (1985). *Keys to solution in brief therapy*. New York: Norton.

de Shazer, S. (1988). *Clues: Investigating solutions in brief therapy*. New York: W. W. Norton.

de Shazer, S. (1991). *Putting difference to work*. New York: Norton.

Duncan, B., Hubble, M., & Miller, S. (Eds.). (1999). *Heart and soul of change: What works in therapy*. Washington, DC: American Psychological Association Press.

Fitzpatrick, M. R., & Stalikas, A. (2008a). Integrating positive emotions into theory, research, and practice: A new challenge for psychotherapy. *Journal of Psychotherapy Integration, 18*, 248–258.

Fitzpatrick, M. R., & Stalikas, A. (2008b). Positive emotions as generators of therapeutic change. *Journal of Psychotherapy Integration, 18*, 137–154.

Franklin, C., & Streeter, C. L. (2004). *Solution-focused accountability schools for the 21st century*. Austin, TX: Hogg Foundation for Mental Health, University of Texas at Austin.

Franklin, C., Biever, J., Moore, K., Clemons, D., & Scamardo, M. (2001). The effectiveness of solution-focused therapy with children in a school setting. *Research on Social Work Practice, 11*(4), 411–434.

Fredrickson, B. L. (1998). What good are positive emotions? *Review of General Psychology, 2*, 300–319.

Garland, E. L., Fredrickson, B., Kring, A. M., Johnson, D. P., Meyer P. S., & Penn, D. L. (2010). Upward spirals of positive emotions counter downward spirals of negativity: Insights from the broaden-and-build theory and affective neuroscience on the treatment of emotion dysfunctions and deficits in psychopathology. *Clinical Psychology Review, 30*, 849–864.

Garner, J. (2004). Creating solution-building schools training program. In C. Franklin & C. L. Streeter (Eds.), *Solution-focused accountability schools for the 21st century*. Austin, TX: Hogg Foundation for Mental Health, University of Texas at Austin.

House, A. (2002). *DSM-IV diagnosis in the schools*. New York: Guilford.

Kim, J. S. (2008). Examining the effectiveness of solution-focused brief therapy: A meta-analysis. *Research on Social Work Practice.*

Kim, J. S. (2014). *Solution-focused brief therapy: A multicultural approach.* Thousand Oaks, CA: Sage Publications.

Kim, J. S., & Franklin, C. (2015). The importance of positive emotions in solution-focused brief therapy. *Best Practices in Mental Health, 11,* 25–41.

Korman, H., Bavelas, J. B., & De Jong, P. (2013). Microanalysis of formulations in solution-focused brief therapy, cognitive behavioral therapy, and motivational interviewing. *Journal of Systemic Therapies, 32,* 31–45.

Lever, N., Anthony, L., Stephan, S., Moore, E., Harrison, B., & Weist, M. (2006). Best practice in expanded school mental health services. In C. Franklin, M. Harris, & P. Allen-Meares (Eds.), *School services source-book* (pp. 1011–1020). New York: Oxford Press.

Lipchik, E. (1994). The rush to be brief. *Family Therapy Networker, 18*(2), 35–39.

MacDonald, A. J. (2007). *Solution-focused therapy: Theory, research and practice.* London: Sage Books.

Metcalf, L. (1995). *Counseling towards solutions: A practical solution-focused program for working with students, teachers, and parents.* New York: Jossey-Bass.

Miller, G., & de Shazer, S. (2000). Emotions in solution-focused therapy: A re-examination. *Family Process, 39*(1), 5–23.

Moskowitz, E. (2001). *In therapy we trust: America's obsession with self-fulfillment.* Baltimore: Johns Hopkins Press.

Murphy, J. (1996). Solution-focused brief therapy in the school. In S. Miller, M. Hubble, & B. Duncan (Eds.), *Handbook of solution-focused brief therapy* (pp. 184–204). San Francisco: Jossey-Bass Publishers.

Newsome, S. (2004). Solution-focused brief therapy (SFBT) group work with at-risk junior high school students: Enhancing the bottom-line. *Research on Social Work Practice, 14*(5), 336–343.

Norcross, J., & Goldried, M. (2003). *Handbook of psychotherapy integration.* New York: Oxford Press.

Nylund, D., & Corsiglia, V. (1994). Becoming solution-focused forced in brief therapy: Remembering something important we already knew. *Journal of Systemic Therapies, 13*(1), 5–12.

O'Hanlon, B., & Bertolino, B. (1998). *Even from a broken web: Brief, respectful solution-oriented therapy for sexual abuse and trauma.* New York: Wiley.

Selekman, M. (2005). *Pathways to change* (2nd ed.). New York: Guilford.

Solution-Focused Brief Therapy Association (2006). SFBT Training Manual. Retrieved July 3, 2007, from http://www.sfbta.org/

Tallman, K., & Bohart, A. (1999). The client as a common factor: Clients as self-healers. In B. Duncan, M. Hubble, & S. Miller (Eds.), *The heart and soul of change: What works in therapy* (pp. 91–132). Washington, DC: American Psychological Association Press.

Wylie, M. (1994, March/April). *Endangered species.* Family Therapy Networker.

3

SFBT and Evidence-Based Practice
The State of the Science

Johnny S. Kim, Michael S. Kelly, & Cynthia Franklin

Introduction

SFBT has become a popular therapy model for social work practice, especially within school settings. Part of the model's appeal to social workers lies in its strengths-based focus. De Jong and Miller (1995) note that social work history is rooted in the principles of the strengths perspective but has lacked specific tools and techniques to put strengths-based practice into action. Building on Saleebey's (1992) summary of strengths-based assumptions and principles, De Jong and Miller (1995) argue that SFBT can advance social work's tradition of using strengths-based principles by providing specific intervention skills and change techniques with similar philosophical assumptions.

Practitioners from many disciplines, but especially social work, have embraced SFBT because of the ease in implementing the model and its flexibility for different practice settings. In an era of accountability and evidence-based practice, however, the effectiveness of SFBT is important for social workers to consider. The chapter summarizes the research support for, and addresses the state of research on, the SFBT model compared to other intervention models. Particular emphasis is given to a meta-analysis of SFBT and to a review of SFBT studies conducted in school settings.

Although SFBT undoubtedly is popular among social workers in the United States and around the world, the research on its effectiveness is still limited in relation to its growing popularity (Gingerich & Eisengart, 2000; Triantafillou, 1997; Zimmerman, Prest, & Wetzel, 1997). This poses problems both for social workers who have embraced the SFBT model and for the schools of social work teaching SFBT as part of their curriculum. Fortunately, research studies are showing that SFBT is an effective intervention, and research on this model continues to grow by the year.

Early Research Studies

Two of the earliest studies on the effectiveness of SFBT were conducted by the team at the Brief Family Therapy Center (BFTC). De Jong and Hopwood (1996) provide an overview of the first study, which was conducted by Kiser (1988) and consisted of follow-up surveys (at 6, 12, and 18 months after termination of therapy) to determine whether clients had met their goals or felt they had made significant progress. Results showed an 80% success rate, with 65.6% meeting their goals and 14.7% feeling they were making significant improvements. At the 18-month follow-up, 86% of the contacted clients reported success. These initial studies showed SFBT to be a promising approach.

The second study, conducted by De Jong and Hopwood (1996), involved 275 clients seen at the BFTC from November 1992 to August 1993. Similar to Kiser's (1988) study, participants were contacted 7 to 9 months after termination of therapy and asked whether they had met their goals. Results from this study indicated that of the 136 participants who responded, 45% reported meeting their goals, 32% reported some progress toward their goals, and 23% reported no progress. On the intermediate score measure, 141 responses were calculated on the basis of the therapists' session notes. Results from this measure showed that 25% reported significant progress, 49% reported moderate progress, and 26% reported no progress. Limitations of this study were similar to those of Kiser's (1988) study because it lacked multiple, standardized measures. Despite the lack of rigorous designs in these two early studies, however, the initial success and positive results were impressive enough to warrant further research on this promising model.

Systematic Reviews

Gingerich and Eisengart (2000) conducted the first systematic, qualitative review of the 15 controlled outcome studies on SFBT up to 1999. All of these studies used either a comparison group or single-case, repeated-measures design to evaluate various client behaviors or functioning. The studies were divided into three groups according to the degree of experimental control employed. Five studies met the well-controlled standard, four studies met the moderately controlled standard, and six studies met the poorly controlled standard.

Recently Gingerich and Peterson (2013) updated this previous systematic review (Gingerich & Eisengart, 2000) and looked at 43 controlled outcome studies on SFBT conducted internationally. Studies were grouped into six different categories: child academic and behavior problems, adult mental health, marriage and family, occupational rehabilitation, health and aging, and crime and delinquency. Overall, results showed that 74% of the studies reported significant positive benefits for those clients receiving SFBT intervention. Of particular interest to school social workers are the 14 studies that looked at child academic and behavior problems. Table 3.1 provides a detailed looked at these studies.

Of the 14 studies that looked at this subgroup, 11 were conducted in school settings, mostly in the United States. Overall, 12 of the studies found improvement in the SFBT group after intervention on all or most outcomes. Only two studies (Cook, 1998; Leggett, 2004) reported no difference in the SFBT group after intervention for most or all outcomes. When examining how the SFBT group compared with the control group, three of the studies (Cepukiene & Pakrosnis, 2011; Franklin, Moore, & Hopson, 2008; Froeschle, Smith, & Ricard, 2007) showed statistically significant differences on all or most outcomes over those students in the control group. An additional three studies (Daki & Savage, 2010; Newsome, 2004; Springer, Lynch, & Rubin, 2000) showed changes in the desired direction for the SFBT group on all or most outcomes. Six studies (Cook, 1998; Corcoran, 2006; Kvarme et al., 2010; Leggett, 2004; Littrell, Malia, & Vanderwood, 1995; Wilmshurst, 2002) did not report any difference between the SFBT and control groups on all or most outcomes. Two studies (Fearrington, McCallum, & Skinner, 2011; Yarbrough, 2004) did not report between-group results because they used a single-group design and did not have a comparison group. Taken together, these studies continue to show the diversity in SFBT application as well as the promising results when using SFBT with children and youth.

Meta-Analysis

The good news is that since Gingerich and Eisengart's (2000) review, more research studies have examined the effectiveness of SFBT. To advance the

Table 3.1 Child Academic and Behavior Problems (Gingerich & Peterson, 2013)

Study	Setting	Sample Size	Duration And Modality	Outcome Measure	SFBT Pre-Post	Comparison Group Contrast
Cepukiene & Pakrosnis (2011)	Foster homes (Lithuania)	46	1–5 sessions, individual counseling	Behavior problems	+*	+*
				Somatic/cognitive problems	+	+
Cook (1998)	School	68	6 sessions, 30-min classroom	Self-concept	0	0
Corcoran (2006)	University clinic	85	4–6 sessions, family counseling	Behavior problems (Conners Parent Rating Scale)	+	0
				Behavior problems (Feelings, Attitudes, and Behaviors Scale for children)	0	0
Daki & Savage (2010)	Learning centers (Canada)	14	5 sessions, 40-min individual counseling	Academic achievement	+	0
				Reading fluency	+	+
				Reading motivation	+	+
				Reading activity inventory	+	0
				Self-esteem	+	+
				Behavioral disorders	+	+

Study	Setting	N	Intervention	Outcome		
Fearrington, McCallum, & Skinner (2011)	Inner-city school	6	5 sessions, 30-min individual counseling	Assignment completion	+	n/a
				Assignment accuracy	+	
Franklin, Moore, & Hopson (2008)	School	53	5–7 sessions, 45-min individual counseling	Child behavior teacher report, externalizing	+	+*
				Child behavior teacher report, internalizing	+	+*
				Child behavior student report, externalizing	+	+*
				Child behavior student report, internalizing	+	0
Froeschle, Smith, & Ricard (2007)	School	65	16 sessions, 1-h group	Drug use	+	+*
				Attitudes	+	+*
				Self-concept	+	0
				Social competence	+	+*
				Social behaviors	+	+*
				Drug knowledge	+	+*
Kvarme et al. (2010)	School (Norway)	144	5 sessions, 1-h group	General self-efficacy	+*	0
				Specific self-efficacy	+	+
				Assertive self-efficacy	+*	0
Leggett (2004)	School	67	11 sessions, 1-h classroom	Self-esteem	+	+
				Hope	0	0
				Classroom environment	0	0

(Continued)

Table 3.1 (Continued)

Study	Setting	Sample Size	Duration And Modality	Outcome Measure	SFBT Pre-Post	Comparison Group Contrast
Littrell, Malia, & Vanderwood (1995)	School	54	1 session, 20- to 50-min individual counseling	Alleviating concerns	+*	0
				Goal attainment	+*	0
				Intensity of feelings	+*	0
Newsome (2004)	School	52	8 sessions, 30-min group	GPA	+*	+
				Attendance	+	+
Springer, Lynch, & Rubin (2000)	School	10	6 sessions, group	Self-esteem	+*	+
Wilmshurst (2002)	Residential program (Canada)	65	12 weeks, 5-day residential program	Emotional/behavioral disorders, externalizing	+*	≈
				Emotional/behavioral disorders, internalizing	0	+*
				Social competence	+*	≈
				Behavior problems	+*	≈
Yarbrough (2004)	School	6	5 sessions, 30-min individual counseling	Assignment completion	+	n/a
				Assignment accuracy	+	

Note. 0 = no difference; + = positive trend in desired direction; +* = statistical significant positive change; ≈ = approximately equal; n/a - not applicable.

research on SFBT and provide an updated review for practitioners, a meta-analysis was conducted by Kim (2008). A *meta-analysis* is a quantitative review method that allows researchers to combine and synthesize existing studies and reanalyze them to determine overall outcomes. The effect size statistic is used to report the outcomes of the review. By calculating effect sizes, the meta-analyst converts measures in primary studies to a common metric of treatment effect or relation between variables. It is possible to achieve small (.30), medium (.50), or large (.80) effect sizes when calculating the outcomes. Most practice research in the social work field typically finds small effect sizes when evaluating an intervention (Kim, 2008). See Box 3.1 for a formal definition and description of meta-analysis.

Kim (2008) synthesized SFBT outcome studies to determine the overall effectiveness of this approach and thus provided more empirical information on its effectiveness. Because these studies vary in regard to research designs, populations, and findings, a research synthesis using meta-analytic

Box 3.1 Description of a Meta-Analysis

A *meta-analysis* integrates findings from a collection of individual studies with similar outcome constructs to determine the magnitude of the treatment effect (Glass, 1976). Instead of relying on anecdotal evidence, meta-analytic procedures can be used to synthesize quantitative results from studies to calculate effect sizes, which measure the strength and direction of a relationship. The larger the magnitude of the effect size, the stronger the treatment effect. Confidence intervals can also be calculated to measure the precision of the effect size estimate. Furthermore, heterogeneity in effect sizes is found across studies, then predictor variables can be examined to help explain this variability (Hall, Tickle-Degnen, Rosenthal, & Mosteller, 1994). The statistical method of meta-analysis has been used to identify effective practice methods developed and evaluated by social workers since the 1980s (Reid, 2002). An SFBT meta-analysis can add to this progress by systematically evaluating the effectiveness of this approach through the aggregation of multiple outcome studies (Corcoran, Miller, & Bultman, 1997).

procedures appears to be a good approach to examine the state of the empirical evidence for SFBT. By calculating effect sizes, Kim's (2008) meta-analysis goes beyond the two systematic reviews discussed earlier (Gingerich & Eisengart, 2000; Gingerich & Peterson, 2013) by using means and standard deviations from the primary studies to come up with overall treatment effects for SFBT.

The main research question for Kim's (2008) meta-analysis was the effectiveness of SFBT for externalizing behavior problems (e.g., aggression and conduct problems), internalizing behavior problems (e.g., depression and self-esteem), and family or relationship problems. These were the most frequent outcomes measured in the studies on SFBT, and they are of considerable interest to social workers. The results from the literature search produced 22 studies that met the criteria for inclusion in the meta-analysis. These 22 studies were then divided and grouped into three categories based on the outcome problem each study targeted (i.e., externalizing behavior problems, internalizing behavior problems, and family and relationship problems). Each of the three categories had between 8 and 12 studies, with 5 studies (Franklin, Moore, & Hopson, 2008; Huang, 2001; Marinaccio, 2001; Seagram, 1997; Triantafillou, 2002) being included in more than one category because they examined more than one outcome problem.

Kim (2008) found that SFBT demonstrated small, but positive, treatment effects favoring the SFBT group on the outcome measures. The overall weighted mean effect size estimates were .13 for externalizing behavior problems, .26 for internalizing problem behaviors, and .26 for family and relationship problems. Only the magnitude of the effect for internalizing behavior problems was statistically significant at the $p < .05$ level, indicating that the treatment outcome for the SFBT group was different from the treatment outcome for the control group.

The small effect sizes calculated in Kim's (2008) meta-analysis are only slightly smaller than other effect sizes calculated in similar social science research. As Table 3.2 highlights, SFBT effect sizes are comparable to those in other psychotherapy and social work meta-analyses when conducted under real-world conditions.

Kim's (2008) meta-analysis did not achieve the medium and large effect sizes for SFBT that researchers like to see in outcomes. As noted, however, it is unusual to achieve anything above a small effect size when evaluating applied research studies in community settings, and this would be the case

Table 3.2 Comparison of Meta-Analyses

Study	Treatment Intervention	Population	Outcome Measure	Effect Size
Kim (2008)	SFBT	Various	Externalizing problems	.13
			Internalizing problems	.26
			Family and relationship problems	.26
Weisz, McCarty, & Valeri (2006)	Psychotherapy (overall)	Adolescents	Depression	.34
	Psychotherapy in real-world clinical setting	Adolescents	Depression	.24
Babcock, Green, & Robie (2004)	Domestic violence treatment	Domestically violent males	Police reports	.18
			Partner reports	.18
Gorey (1996)	General social work practice	Various	Various	.36

with SFBT research as well. To illustrate, the small effect sizes calculated in the SFBT meta-analysis are only slightly smaller than the effect sizes calculated for psychotherapy. For example, psychotherapy's mean overall effect size on adolescent depression, when including dissertations and using more rigorous effect size calculations than previous meta-analyses on this subject, was a moderate .34, with a range of –.66 to 2.02 (Weisz, McCarty, & Valeri, 2006). In addition, studies on the effectiveness of psychotherapy on adolescent depression that were conducted in real-world settings had a small overall weighted mean effect size of .24. Similarly, Babcock, Green, and Robie (2004) cite other meta-analyses on psychotherapy with small effect size results due to difficulties in treating externalizing problem behaviors like aggression (Loesel & Koeferl, 1987; Weisz, Weiss, Han, Granger, & Morton, 1995). Therefore, while Kim's (2008) study found small treatment effects for SFBT, other meta-analyses on psychotherapy have found only slightly better or equal results, depending on the research study setting.

Current Research in School Settings

While the preceding section focused primarily on SFBT research overall, several recent studies have focused on SFBT in school settings. The application of SFBT with students and in school settings has grown over the past 15 years and continues to be an area of interest for researchers, school social workers, and other school-based professionals. SFBT has been applied in school settings to a number of problems, including student behavioral and emotional issues, academic problems, and social skills. Recently, Kim and Franklin (2009) reviewed the outcome literature on SFBT in schools. Table 3.3 summarizes the most rigorous experimental and quasi-experimental design studies on SFBT in schools that have been published in peer-reviewed journals, some of which overlap with those noted in the Gingerich and Peterson (2013) study.

As Table 3.3 highlights, six experimental design studies and one single-case design study on SFBT in schools have been published since 2000. The results from most of the studies were mixed, thereby limiting the ability to draw definitive conclusions. Initial impressions of these results may be misleading, however, as the authors of the studies note several factors that may have influenced the mixed results.

These types of mixed results are not unusual for studies conducted in real-world practice settings (viz., effectiveness study), which are more common in social work research, as opposed to research studies conducted in clinical settings (viz., efficacy studies), which are more common in psychology. Efficacy studies conducted in clinical settings are able to control for many factors, such as intervention training, treatment fidelity, and client selection, that effectiveness studies conducted in practical settings are not (Connor-Smith & Weisz, 2003). A major problem with efficacy studies, however, is the diminished results found when models are transferred from the clinical setting to real-world settings such as schools (Southam-Gerow, Weisz, & Kendall, 2003; Weisz, 2004). In contrast, all of the studies in Table 3.3 were conducted in real-world settings and therefore show promise under typical clinical practice situations, unlike the optimal clinical efficacy studies that have been shown to be ineffective when the model is transferred into clinical practice settings (Kim, 2008).

An important feature in these recent studies is the positive results found in almost all of them for those students receiving SFBT. These positive outcomes suggest that solution-focused therapy can be beneficial in helping

Table 3.3 SFBT Studies in Schools (Kim & Franklin, 2009)

Study	Design	Outcome Measure	Sample Size	Sample Population	Results
Corcoran (2006)	Quasi-experimental	Conners Parent Rating Scale; Feelings, Attitudes, and Behaviors Scale for Children	86	Students aged 5–17 years	No significant differences between groups, with both improving at posttest. This lack of difference may be because the comparison group received treatment as usual, which had many CBT components that have been empirically validated.
Franklin Biever, Moore, Clemons, & Scamardo (2001)	Single case	Conners Teacher Rating Scale	7	Middle school students aged 10–12 years	Five of seven (71%) improved per teacher reports.

(Continued)

Table 3.3 (Continued)

Study	Design	Outcome Measure	Sample Size	Sample Population	Results
Franklin, Streeter, Kim, & Tripodi (2007)	Quasi-experimental	Grades and attendance	85	At-risk high school students	SFBT sample had statistically significant higher average proportion of credits earned to credits attempted than the comparison sample. Both groups decreased in mean attendance per semester; however, the comparison group showed a higher proportion of school days attended to school days for the semester. Authors suggested that attendance between groups may not be a fair comparison because the SFBT group worked on a self-paced curriculum and could decrease their attendance when completed.

Franklin, Moore, & Hopson (2008)	Quasi-experimental	Child Behavior Checklist (CBCL) Youth Self-Report Form Internalizing; CBCL Externalizing; Teacher's Report Form internalizing and externalizing score	59	Middle school students	Internalizing and externalizing score for the Teacher's Report Form showed the SFBT group declined below clinical level by posttest and remained there at follow-up, whereas the comparison group changed little. Internalizing score for the Youth Self-Report Form showed no difference between groups. Externalizing score showed the SFBT group dropped below the clinical level and continued to drop at follow-up.
Froeschle, Smith, & Ricard (2007)	Experimental design	American Drug & Alcohol Survey; Substance Abuse Subtle Screening Inventory; knowledge on physical symptoms of drug use; Piers-Harris Children's Self-Concept Scale; Home & Community Social Behavior Scales; School Social Behavior Scales; referrals; and GPA	65	Eighth-grade female students	Statistically significant differences were found favoring the SFBT group on drug use, attitudes toward drugs, knowledge of physical symptoms of drug use, and competent behavior scores as observed by both parents and teachers. No group differences were found on self-esteem, negative behaviors as measured by office referrals, and GPAs.

(Continued)

Table 3.3 (Continued)

Study	Design	Outcome Measure	Sample Size	Sample Population	Results
Newsome (2004)	Quasi-experimental	Grades and attendance	52	Middle school students	Statistically significant results, with the SFBT group increasing mean grade scores, whereas the comparison group's grades decreased. No difference on attendance measure.
Springer, Lynch, & Rubin (2000)	Quasi-experimental	Hare Self-Esteem Scale	10	Hispanic elementary school students	The SFBT group made significant improvements on the Hare Self-Esteem Scale, whereas the comparison group's scores remained the same. However, no significant differences were found between the SFBT and comparison groups at the end of the study on the self-esteem scale.

students reduce the intensity of their negative feelings, manage their conduct problems, improve academic outcomes like credits earned, and positively impact externalizing behavior problems and substance use (Kim & Franklin, 2009). Although at present there may not be enough studies to draw definitive conclusions about the effectiveness of SFBT, the use of rigorous research designs in real-world settings with increased sample sizes and statistical power does provide support for looking upon it as a promising therapy model. In fact, all the studies described in Table 3.3 use either an experimental or quasi-experimental design, which helps reduce threats to internal validity (Rubin & Babbie, 2005). The more recent outcome studies on SFBT have moved beyond follow-up survey studies of the past and begun to employ more rigorous, well-controlled study designs, lending even more credibility to interpretations of the results obtained. In fact, viewed practically, SFBT is offered with only a few clinical sessions and has been shown to perform in a manner similar to other therapeutic approaches conducted in community settings with longer therapy sessions.

Research Implications for Practice in Schools

When the first edition of this book was published, the state of the research on SFBT and the limited numbers of studies available provided only tentative answers about the effectiveness of SFBT in school settings. Those early, positive findings for internalizing and behavioral outcomes, however, may have considerable clinical significance for school-based practitioners because of the effect sizes achieved and the fact that most of the studies involved salient issues for school practitioners (e.g., conduct problems, hyperactivity, or substance use). Since then, much has changed, not only in terms of the number of research studies conducted on SFBT but also in the perception of SFBT as an evidence-based intervention. There is less talk or debate about whether SFBT is evidence based due to the increase in outcome studies from around the world showing its effectiveness (Franklin, Trepper, Gingerich, & McCollum, 2012). In addition, SFBT has been listed on the Substance Abuse and Mental Health Services Administration National Registry of Evidence-Based Programs and Practices site as an evidence-based intervention.

SFBT may be beneficial for those difficult clients who have been unsuccessful in resolving problems using other, more typical approaches. For example, Franklin et al. (2008) conducted a study in a school setting with children who were having classroom and behavior problems that could not be resolved by teachers and principals. The students underwent individual sessions of SFBT combined with teacher consultations. After receiving the SFBT intervention, teachers reported on a standardized measure (Conners Teacher Rating Scale) that the children's behavior problems significantly improved. Children also rated themselves and reported that their behavior had improved. The effect sizes were medium to large for the changes achieved.

Another advantage of SFBT for social work practice is that this model can help to create change in the target problem quickly and can identify specific goals collaborated on by both the client and the social worker. Across the three different outcome categories reported in the Franklin et al. meta-analysis, several individual studies found large effect sizes with six or fewer therapy sessions (Cockburn, Thomas, & Cockburn, 1997; Franklin et al., 2008; Sundstrom, 1993). Furthermore, many of the studies examining the effectiveness of SFBT were conducted in real-world settings and therefore show promise under typical practice situations—again, unlike the optimal clinical efficacy studies, which have shown to be ineffective when the model is transferred into clinical practice settings.

Although this chapter has focused on examining the state of the research on SFBT and its effectiveness, keep in mind that many common factors play an important role in treatment effectiveness. These common factors are less about specific techniques and more about the therapeutic relationship and individual characteristics that help bring about change in clients. These factors focus more on the personality and behavior of social workers, expectations of change, and engagement in therapy-relevant activities (Kazdin, 2005). Therefore, trying to determine whether SFBT is more effective than other therapy models may prove futile: some studies have shown that many therapies are basically equal in effectiveness, and other non-treatment factors common across therapy models may bring about therapeutic change independent of the social worker's specific techniques (Lambert, 2005; Reisner, 2005; Wampold, 2001). What is more essential in research is for SFBT to demonstrate superiority to some control condition or group of clients who received treatment-as-usual or received no treatment (Chambless, 2002; Duncan, Miller, & Sparks, 2004).

Concerns also arise about the evaluation of treatment fidelity by the therapists conducting the SFBT sessions and their training level in the model. Do these practitioners know how to do SFBT, and how well did they do it in the sessions? Results on the effectiveness of SFBT could be misleading if practitioners aren't adequately trained or do not adhere to the core components of the therapy model. One possible approach to improving treatment fidelity in outcome research studies is utilizing a treatment manual to further improve adherence to the SFBT model. However, using a treatment manual has not been demonstrated to improve practice to a great extent in the real world (Duncan et al., 2004). Most therapy models that are deemed to be evidence based, however, are manualized practices that provide some consistency among researchers conducting the studies. Currently, the Solution-Focused Brief Therapy Association in North America and the European Brief Therapy Association have created treatment manuals that will aid in improving intervention fidelity. The introduction of these manuals demonstrates that SFBT adherents are getting serious about training and fidelity on the model. An excerpt from the treatment manual developed by the Solution-Focused Brief Therapy Association is shown in Box 3.2. Improving treatment fidelity in future studies, and making sure that clinicians conducting SFBT sessions

---

Box 3.2 SFBT Manual Excerpt

Therapist Characteristics and Requirements

SFBT therapists should posses the requisite training and certification in mental health discipline, and specialized training in SFBT. The ideal SFBT therapist would posses (a) a minimum of a master's degree in a counseling discipline such as counseling, social work, marriage and family therapy, psychology, or psychiatry; (b) formal training and supervision in solution-focused therapy, either via a university class or a series of workshops and training experiences as well as supervision in their settings. Therapists who seem to embrace and excel as solution focused therapists have these characteristics: (a) are warm and friendly; (b) Are naturally positive and supportive (often are told they "see the good in people"); (c) are open minded and flexible to new ideas; (d) are excellent listeners, especially the ability to listen for clients' previous solutions embedded in "problem-talk"; and (e) are tenacious and patient.

(Bavelas et al., 2013, p. 23)

---

have extensive training in the SFBT model, will help ensure confidence in the results obtained from the primary study.

To confidently determine the effectiveness of SFBT through a meta-analytic review, more primary studies with larger sample sizes and rigorous research designs are required. In addition, studies using experimental designs need to utilize standardized measures that are sensitive enough to measure brief intervention changes and that possess satisfactory clinical sensitivity, especially for internalizing behavior problems. To help reduce the number of studies excluded from meta-analysis, reported studies should include enough statistical information to calculate effect sizes, such as means and standard deviations, for both pretest and posttest groups as well as experimental and control groups.

Summary

This chapter summarized the research support for SFBT and addressed the state of the research on SFBT as compared to other intervention models. Particular emphasis was given to reviewing a meta-analysis on SFBT conducted by Kim (2008) as well as other, more recent systematic reviews of SFBT studies conducted in school settings. The research on SFBT has steadily grown over the years, and this therapy model is now viewed as evidence based. The studies that exist consistently demonstrate that SFBT is a promising, effective approach that is useful for students in school settings and for community service providers.

References

Babcock, J. C., Green, C. E., & Robie, C. (2004). Does batterers' treatment work? A meta-analytic review of domestic violence treatment. *Clinical Psychology Review*, 23, 1023–1053.

Bavelas, J., De Jong, P., Franklin, C., Froerer, A., Gingerich, W., Kim, J., Korman, H., Langer, S., Lee, M. Y., McCollum, E. E., Smock Jordan, S., & Trepper, T. S. (2013, July 1). Solution focused therapy treatment manual for working with individuals, 2nd version. Retrieved from http://www.sfbta.org/researchdownloads.html

Cepukiene, V., & Pakrosnis, R. (2011). The outcome of solution-focused brief therapy among foster care adolescents: The changes of behavior and perceived somatic and cognitive difficulties. *Children and Youth Services Review*, 33, 791–797.

Chambless, D. L. (2002). Beware the Dodo bird: The dangers of overgeneralization. *Clinical Psychology: Science and Practice*, 9, 13–19.

Cockburn, J. T., Thomas, F. N., & Cockburn, O. J. (1997). Solution-focused therapy and psychosocial adjustment to orthopedic rehabilitation in a work hardening program. *Journal of Occupational Rehabilitation, 7,* 97–106.

Connor-Smith, J. K., & Weisz, J. R. (2003). Applying treatment outcome research in clinical practice: Techniques for adapting interventions to the real world. *Child and Adolescent Mental Health, 8,* 3–10.

Cook, D. R. (1998). *Solution-focused brief therapy: Its impact on the self-concept of elementary school students.* Unpublished Dissertation, Ohio University, Athens, Ohio.

Corcoran, J. (2006). A comparison group study of solution-focused therapy versus "treatment-as-usual" for behavior problems in children. *Journal of Social Service Research, 33*(1), 69–81.

Corcoran, J., Miller, P., & Bultman, L. (1997). Effectiveness of prevention programs for adolescent pregnancy: A meta analysis. *Journal of Marriage and the Family, 59,* 551–567.

Daki, J., & Savage, R. (2010). Solution-focused brief therapy: Impacts on academic and emotional difficulties. *Journal of Educational Research, 103,* 309–326.

De Jong, P., & Hopwood, L. E. (1996). Outcome research on treatment conducted at the Brief Family Therapy Center, 1992–1993. In S. D. Miller, M. A. Hubble, & B. L. Duncan (Eds.), *Handbook of solution-focused brief therapy* (pp. 272–298). San Francisco: Jossey Bass.

De Jong, P., & Miller, S. D. (1995). How to interview for client strengths. *Social Work, 40*(6), 729–736.

Duncan, B. L., Miller, S. D., & Sparks, J. (2004). *The heroic client: A radical way to improve effectiveness through client-directed, outcome informed therapy.* San Francisco: Jossey-Bass.

Fearrington, J. Y., McCallum, R. S., & Skinner, C. H. (2011). Increasing math assignment completion using solution-focused brief counseling. *Education and Treatment of Children, 34,* 61–80.

Franklin, C., Biever, J., Moore, K., Clemons, D., & Scamardo, M. (2001). The effectiveness of solution-focused therapy with children in a school setting. *Research on Social Work Practice, 11*(4), 411–434.

Franklin, C., Streeter, C. L., Kim, J. S., & Tripodi, S. J. (2007). The effectiveness of a solution-focused, public alternative school for dropout prevention and retrieval. *Children & Schools, 29,* 133–144.

Franklin, C., Moore, K., & Hopson, L.M. (2008). Effectiveness of solution-focused brief therapy in a school setting. *Children & Schools, 30,* 15–26.

Franklin, C., Trepper, T., Gingerich, W. McCollum, E. (2012). *Solution-focused brief therapy: A handbook of evidence based practice.* New York: Oxford University Press.

Froeschle, J. G., Smith, R. L., & Ricard, R. (2007). The efficacy of a systematic substance abuse program for adolescent females. *Professional School Counseling, 10,* 498–505.

Gingerich, W., & Eisengart, S. (2000). Solution-focused brief therapy: A review of outcome research. *Family Process, 39*(4), 477–496.

Gingerich, W. J. & Peterson, L. T. (2013). Effectiveness of solution-focused brief therapy: A systematic qualitative review of controlled outcome studies. *Research on Social Work Practice, 23,* 266–283.

Glass, G. V. (1976). Primary, secondary, and meta-analysis. *Educational Researcher*, 5, 3–8.

Gorey, K. M. (1996). Effectiveness of social work intervention research: Internal versus external evaluations. *Social Work*, 7, 63–80.

Hall, J. A., Tickle-Degnen, L., Rosenthal, R., & Mosteller, F. (1994). Hypotheses and problems in research synthesis. In H. Cooper & L. V. Hedges (Eds.), *The Handbook of research synthesis* (pp. 17–28). New York: Russell Sage Foundation.

Huang, M. (2001). *A comparison of three approaches to reduce marital problems and symptoms of depression*. Unpublished Dissertation. University of Florida.

Daki & Savage, 2010

Kazdin, E. (2005). Treatment outcomes, common factors, and continued neglect of mechanisms of change. *Clinical Psychology: Science and Practice*, 12(2), 184–188.

Kim, J. S. (2008). Examining the effectiveness of solution-focused brief therapy: A meta-analysis. *Research on Social Work Practice*.

Kim, J. S., & Franklin, C. (2009). Solution-focused, brief therapy in schools: A review of the outcome literature. *Children and Youth Services Review*, 31, 464–470.

Kiser, D. (1988). *A follow-up study conducted at the brief family therapy center*. Unpublished manuscript.

Kvarme, L. G., Helseth, S., Sorum, R., Luth-Hansen, V., Haugland, S., & Natvig, G. K. (2010). The effect of a solution-focused approach to improve self-efficiacy in socially withdrawn school children: A non-randomized controlled trial. *International Journal of Nursing Studies*, 47, 1389–1396.

Lambert, M. J. (2005). Early response in psychotherapy: Further evidence for the importance of common factors rather than placebo effects. *Journal of Clinical Psychology*, 6(1), 855–869.

Leggett, M. E. S. (2004). *The effects of a solution-focused classroom guidance intervention with elementary students*. Unpublished Dissertation, Texas A&M University-Corpus Christi, Corpus Christi, Texas.

Littrell, J. M., Malia, J. A., & Vanderwood, M. (1995). Single-session brief counseling in a high school. *Journal of Counseling and Development*, 73, 451–458.

Loesel, F., & Koeferl, P. (1987). Evaluation research on the social-therapeutic prison: A meta-analysis. *Gruppendynamik*, 18, 385–406.

Marinaccio, B. C. (2001). *The effects of school-based family therapy*. Unpublished Dissertation. University of New York at Buffalo.

Newsome, S. (2004). Solution-focused brief therapy (SFBT) group work with at-risk junior high school students: Enhancing the bottom-line. *Research on Social Work Practice*, 14(5), 336–343.

Reid, W. J. (2002). Knowledge for direct social work practice: An analysis of trend. *Social Service Review*, 770(1), 6–33.

Reisner, A. D. (2005). Common factors, empirically validated treatments, and recovery models of therapeutic change. *The Psychological Record*, 55, 377–399.

Rubin, A., & Babbie, E. (2005). *Research methods for social work* (5th ed.). Belmont, CA: Brooks/Cole-Thomson Learning.

Saleebey, D. (1992). *The strengths perspective in social work practice*. New York: Longman.

Seagram, B. M. C. (1997). *The efficacy of solution-focused therapy with young offenders.* Unpublished dissertation. York University (Canada).

Southam-Gerow, M. A., Weisz, J. R., & Kendall, P. C. (2003). Youth with anxiety disorders in research and service clinics: Examining client differences and similarities. *Journal of Clinical Child and Adolescent Psychology, 32*(3), 375–385.

Springer, D. W., Lynch, C., & Rubin, A. (2000). Effects of a solution-focused mutual aid group for Hispanic children of incarcerated parents. *Child & Adolescent Social Work Journal, 17*(6), 431–432.

Sundstrom, S. M. (1993). *Single-session psychotherapy for depression: Is it better to be problem-focused or solution-focused?* Unpublished dissertation. Iowa State University.

Triantafillou, N. (1997). A solution-focused approach to mental health supervision. *Journal of Systemic Therapies, 16*(4), 305–328.

Triantafillou, N. (2002). *Solution-focused parent groups: A new approach to the treatment of youth disruptive behavior.* Unpublished Dissertation. University of Toronto.

Wampold, B. E. (2001). The great psychotherapy debate: Models, methods and findings. Mahwah, NJ: Erlbaum.

Weisz, J. R. (2004). *Psychotherapy for children and adolescents: Evidence-based treatments and case examples.* Cambridge: Cambridge University Press.

Weisz, J. R., McCarty, C. A., & Valeri, S. M. (2006). Effects of psychotherapy for depression in children and adolescents: A meta-analysis. *Psychological Bulletin, 132*(1), 132–149.

Weisz, J. R., Weiss, B., Han, S. S., Granger, D. A., & Morton, T. (1995). Effects of psychotherapy with children and adolescents revisited: A meta- analysis of treatment outcome studies. *Psychological Bulletin, 117*, 450–468.

Wilmshurst, L. A. (2002). Treatment programs for youth with emotional and behavioral disorders: An outcome study of two alternate approaches. *Mental Health Services Research, 4*, 85–96.

Yarbrough, J. L. (2004). *Efficacy of solution-focused brief counseling on math assignment completion and accuracy in an elementary school* (Unpublished Dissertation). University of Tennessee, TN.

Zimmerman, T. S., Prest, L. A., & Wetzel, B. E. (1997). Solution-focused couples therapy groups: An empirical study. *Journal of Family Therapy, 19*(2), 125–144.

4

▨ ▨ ▨

SFBT Within the Tier I Framework
Alternative Schools Adopting the SFBT Model

Cynthia Franklin & Samantha Guz

This chapter discusses the Response-to-Intervention (RtI) framework and how to use SFBT within a Tier 1 (schoolwide) intervention approach with at-risk students. Specifically, this chapter describes how the solution-focused approach is used as a schoolwide intervention within Gonzalo Garza Independence High School in Austin, Texas. A public, alternative school of choice, Garza High School is operated by the Austin Independent School District (AISD). This school is a part of the school district's dropout prevention programs but is also incorporated as a non-profit organization. Garza High School has utilized a solution-focused model since 2002 and has achieved academic success at educating students who are frequently served by school social workers. Most of the students have many risk factors, such as serious social problems (e.g., homelessness, pregnant and parenting, and traumatic experiences) as well as behavioral health challenges (e.g., substance use and mental health diagnoses). In particular, behavioral health challenges are serious concerns to most school districts, and Garza High School has focused most on educating students with these types of problems. Garza has also achieved status as an effective, model school program whose academic achievements and practices have been recognized by the Texas Education Agency and the US Department of Education. This makes Garza High School an excellent choice to discuss because the program shows how solution-focused techniques can become part of a Tier 1 approach within educational programs designed to graduate students who have high-risk factors associated with their behavioral health, family, and community functioning. At Garza High School, all school administrators, teachers, and staff members are trained in SFBT principles of change and techniques to aid in their engagement and work with students.

Tier 1 Approach

Over the past 15 years, campuses have utilized a three-tier system to meet the needs of their diverse student populations: universal (Tier 1), selective (Tier 2), and intensive (Tier 3) interventions. The majority of students (95% or more) have their needs meet by the first two tiers (Sabatino, Kelly, Moriarity, & Lean, 2013). For a school considering the three-tier RtI system, it is important to understand all the tiers while keeping in mind that the most students will respond to the first two levels of intervention. Tier 1 is particularly important because, after receiving the first tier of the RtI, 85% of students will not require any higher level of intervention. The success of Tier 1 is due to the high-quality instruction students received in the classroom, which is designed to prevent future problematic behaviors. The behaviors taught inside the classroom are reinforced throughout the entire school by a variety of staff members. While thought of mainly as an approach to be implemented in primary prevention within all schools, the practices embedded within Tier 1 can also be implemented to create effective school programs that may target one or more groups of students such as those at high risk of dropout.

Graduating students with high-risk profiles requires a team that operates across the entire school to create a safe environment with a climate and culture that will make interventions effective. Teachers, counselors, social workers, or other school-based professionals normally implement Tier 1 in classrooms. This classroom-based implementation helps Tier 1 be campuswide and reach each student. Although qualified school-based professionals lead the instruction in the classroom, the entire school staff is invested in implementing the interventions. A solution-focused approach can be incorporated into a Tier 1 intervention because SFBT engages all of the adults surrounding the student and uses SFBT change processes to support the student's goals. This campuswide dedication is linked to the fidelity of a Tier 1 intervention's implementation. Research suggests campuses that implement Tier 1 interventions with high fidelity have fewer behavioral referrals and, overall, more positive campus climates (Allen-Meares, Montgomery, & Kim, 2013). To maintain the high quality of instruction, assessment, and screening that is required of Tier 1 interventions, the school staff must be trained and involved in the intervention in a way that is meaningful to them.

To accomplish meaningful involvement of staff in an intervention, staff members must be equipped and supported to implement the interventions. Staff also must believe in the credibility and effectiveness of the interventions they are delivering. This requires a professional development approach that allows collaboration between staff, administrators, researchers, and trainers that will ultimately lead to ownership of the interventions. This was the type of training model implemented at Garza High School when they adopted the SFBT approach. All staff within the school received training in ongoing process for two years that included direct instruction from experts on SFBT, video and live demonstrations, and practice with feedback.

Designing a Solution-Focused School Using a Tier 1 Approach

Within Garza High School, SFBT became a campuswide effort to support at-risk students in their efforts toward their graduation. An essential component of this Tier 1 approach was that all teachers and staff become trained in SFBT principles of change and techniques. School-based mental health professionals such as social workers are essential to the success of a Tier 1 approach; however; it is teachers who spend the majority of time with students. With professional development training, teachers can become proficient in mental health techniques and feel confident using them (Franklin, Kim, Ryan, Kelly, & Montgomery, 2012). This was the training philosophy implemented at Garza High School: train the teachers and all the staff to be partners in the change process because schools will never get enough social workers and counselors to meet all the needs. In fact, training all staff actually freed social workers and counselors to do more in-depth counseling and to create needed groups and community linkages while at the same time supporting staff in consultations, training, and work with the students who required additional assistance in the classroom. One of the Garza High School teachers said this about the training philosophy:

> It was the principal's philosophy to train the entire school. Data clerk people were in there, registrars, custodians, because she said anyone can be an advocate. Our custodian is so involved with a lot of our kids and has been a huge advocate and role model for a lot of our kids. He does citywide basketball and recruits some of our kids for that. He talks with them about

manners and accountability; it's just amazing. Anyone can be an [advocate]. A kid may bond with the cafeteria person, so that person needs to be trained like everyone else.

An interprofessional approach was used to train and adapt the SFBT approach to Garza High School. School social workers, counselors, teachers, and administrators melded their areas of expertise into a unique application of solution building. In such an approach, different team members share their knowledge and expertise with one another and create new methods for intervention by adapting that knowledge. Streeter and Franklin (2002) called this learning across disciplinary boundaries a transdisciplinary team approach to solving problems. First, all school staff were trained in the solution-focused, mental health approach to provide the staff better skills for working with at-risk students. In turn, and over time, the school staff adapted the SFBT principles of change and techniques to their educational setting. Staff were encouraged, for example, to adapt the change principles and practices of SFBT to fit the daily challenges in teaching in the classroom and the specific problems they encountered with students (e.g., attendance, tardiness, lack of progress, suicidal ideation, and substance use at school). The specific adaptation was not done by consultants or researchers but, rather, through the creative work of all the staff involved in the school. The way SFBT was being used at Garza was then discussed in subsequent meetings and trainings so that everyone involved continued to learn. Importantly, students were also part of the team effort in developing approaches. As a solution-building school, listening to students and taking their suggestions became a part of the culture. Students were invited to the SFBT trainings, for example, and the principal also convened a principal's advisory group where students were asked to provide ideas about practices within the school.

All staff were trained in SFBT techniques, such as solution-talk, focusing on strengths and exceptions, scaling, and goal setting. Specific principles of change were emphasized, such as the importance of using positive language as means to help someone think about the self and others differently and of setting client-centered goals as essential for the beginning of any change process. Goals, for example, were to be developed collaboratively with students and to be small, measurable, and observable to school staff and parents (Newsome, 2005). School staff also learned the SFBT principle for change that goals are personal and therefore intrinsically motivating for both staff and students (Jones et al., 2009). Administrators and counselors were further encouraged to institutionalize these practices into the school's academic instruction and programs (e.g., daily scaling and goals sheets) and even a special graduation ceremony, called a Star Walk, which is described in more detail later in this chapter.

As noted, the process of learning the philosophy of change and practicing SFBT techniques at Garza High School went on for two years, but in actuality, the professional development and learning about SFBT has never stopped. Once the initial two-year training was accomplishment, ongoing consultations, usually once or twice a semester, continued the transdisciplinary team approach toward adaptation of the solution-focused model to the entire school. At the beginning of training, the original experts on SFBT served as trainers, consultants, evaluators, and scribes of this process, documenting this work in research and in a training manual about the practices. While this may seem like a time-consuming approach to training staff how to use SFBT in a school, it also resulted in the school staff being more competent in SFBT and able to own and, later, take over the training and maintenance of the approach with only minimal consultations from the researchers and trainers, making sure that everyone, including the new teachers, were trained.

The SFBT at Garza High School has been sustained for the past 15 years, including across one change in principal leadership of the school. When the change in leadership occurred in 2008 and founding principal Victoria Baldwin retired, some predicted the SFBT model would not be continued. Ms. Baldwin, however, was involved in selecting Dr. Linda Webb as the new principal, and she not only maintained the SFBT approach but further improved the curriculum and the academic achievement of the school. When Dr. Webb first assumed her position, one of the original trainers became more involved again in the training functions. At this point, Dr. Webb has been thoroughly trained in SFBT and, along with her staff, personally leads the ongoing in-service trainings on the SFBT approach while the original researchers and trainers maintain a consultation and support role. The advantages of training all the teachers and staff in the principles of change and techniques of SFBT, and of encouraging them to adapt the approach to the educational setting, made it easier for the Tier 1 intervention to be implemented at high fidelity (Franklin, Kim, Ryan, Kelly, & Montgomery, 2012). By providing in-depth training in SFBT strategies to everyone at the school, the Tier 1 intervention also became more effective and had more

Table 4.1 Interprofessional Training of School Staff on SFBT

- Obtain support from administration.
- Identify one person to be primarily responsible for training and adherence.
- Create strong partnerships with selected school staff.
- Assess what the school is already doing to build solutions.
- Introduce the model through an interdisciplinary team structure.
- Seek input from all constituents, especially students.
- Maintain a school focus in solution-building conversations.
- Provide opportunities for training by an expert in solution-focused therapy.
- Supporting educators in shaping the model with their own unique philosophy and approach.

Source: Franklin and Streeter (2004).

long-term stability. Table 4.1 summarizes the interprofessional, Tier 1 training approach used at Garza High School.

Solution-Building Approach for At-Risk Students

Garza High School's administrators and staff used the solution-focused techniques to facilitate positive relationships with students and solve problems. Teachers were trained to view students as experts in identifying their own solutions to their problems and difficulties. This view is opposed to the usual approach of expert-driven strategies, and it was discovered that teachers use the solution-building approach more when they can implement SFBT during everyday conversations with students in their own classrooms. Here are some ways that Garza's teachers used the solution-building intervention skills to help students:

- Assisting students to come up with a realistic solution.
- Looking for ways in which the solution is already occurring in the life of the student.
- Assisting the student with creating small, measurable goals toward the solution.
- Taking immediate steps impact educational and life outcomes (Franklin, Montgomery, Baldwin & Webb, 2012).

As discussed in Chapter 3, the use of SFBT in schools has been shown to be a promising intervention (Kim & Franklin, 2009). Garza students display behaviors that may be challenging for teachers, and we now discuss how the solution-focused approach is used to address some common challenges within Garza High School: suicide, self-harm, violence, and aggression.

Suicide and Self-Harm

A solution-focused approach helps teachers and staff builds strong relationships with students (Lagana-Riordan et al., 2011), which are very useful when working with students in stressful situations. In an alternative high school, this relationship is especially essential as multiple students on campus may be at imminent risk of self-harm or suicide. Garza teachers will notice immediately when a student stops attending class or begins behaving atypically. Social workers are available to assist if a student is having a serious mental health crisis that the teacher cannot handle, and the two professionals work as a team to maintain the student in the classroom.

Box 4.1 describes a student who is struggling with mental health and self-harm challenges. In this case, Garza teachers and staff use a team approach and SFBT to support the student, and part of Garza's Tier 1 SFBT approach is a referral system where any staff member can submit a form about any student to a school counselor. These referrals are addressed at a weekly student services meeting. The administration at Garza will create a diverse Student Services Team consisting of teachers, counselors, outside community agencies, and the Communities In Schools social workers. The team works to better understand the students so that they can help students create reasonable goals for themselves. In Maya's case, a safety plan was created and shared with Garza's staff. This type of safety plan would involve a staff member meeting Maya in the morning and after school. In a different school setting, a safety plan could be embarrassing; however, Garza works to destigmatize behavioral health challenges. This is also part of the strengths-based SFBT model, focusing on future possibilities rather than on the past.

As a social worker at Garza who saw students for the 2015–2016 school year said:

> I am amazed at how easily the students tell me about their struggles and trust that I will support and help them. The biggest thing about Garza is how it squashes stigma surrounding so many issues that society battles with today—gender and sexuality, mental health, abuse, learning disabilities, delinquent behavior, citizenship and immigration, and poverty. No matter what is happening in a student's life, they truly know that someone at school will sit down, listen and work hard to help.

Box 4.1 Maya: Suicide Risk

Maya enrolled in Garza High School a few months ago. Since then, she built a strong relationship with her art teacher and become a part of Garza's community. However, Maya is struggling with her mental health again; she had been previously hospitalized for self-harm and suicidal ideation. In the hospital, Maya was diagnosed as Bipolar 1 with a medium level of severity.

Suddenly, Maya's art teacher noticed a change in her. Maya's behavior and mental attitude seemed different; Maya began skipping school and reported engaging in highly risky behaviors. The art teacher filled out a referral and turned it into the school counselor. The referral form was brought to the Student Services Team, an interprofessional team of Garza staff members. At this meeting, they brainstormed Maya's progress at Garza and ways to better support her. During the meeting, the team also recognized the things Maya was doing well: she had been doing well in school, making new friends, and socializing appropriately at home. By listing these strengths, the staff remembered that Maya had the potential to meet future self-assigned goals. Ultimately, due to the past hospitalization and diagnosis, the Garza staff put Maya on a safety plan.

The safety plan was given to all staff on campus along with a picture of Maya so that they could identify her, even if they had never met her. Maya was not seeing an outside therapist; therefore, she was referred to Garza's on campus Communities In Schools (CIS) staff. Maya began seeing the CIS social workers weekly. It was a place where adults were honest and respectful. Even at times when she was worried about her own mental health state, Maya never felt stigmatized on campus.

This quote encapsulates the common challenges facing Garza's student body and how the relational and strengths-based approach of the SFBT permeates the school. All challenges are always framed in an SFBT approach, with a focus on relationships, strengths, and the future solutions that can be taken to make a difference and solve problems.

The school uses the Student Services Team to help create this inclusive culture at Garza. All staff can refer any student to the team. In these weekly meetings, the student's photo is projected, and the team reviews the student's pattern of attendance and behavior in conjunction with what is happening with the student outside of school. The team used a solution-focused approach to remain on task and create small, measurable goals. In the case of Maya, got example, the Student Services Team used compliments to validate what she was doing well.

It is common for the same student to be referred to the team every week. In these situations, the team may decide to keep an eye on this student or consider a more in-depth intervention. The point of these meetings is to understand rather than "fix" the student. To best understand the student's experience, the team is made up of individuals, all staff at Garza, who are diverse in terms of race, age, employment, educational background, LGBT status, and gender. Rather than being held down by frustration, the Student Services Team looks at the referred student to see what has been working and invites the student to do more of that. This technique is strengths based and allows the team to function for the benefit of the students' goals.

Violence and Aggression

Even when disciplining students, the administration takes a solution-building approach, and perhaps this contributes to why Garza High School has so few disciplinary referrals. Violence is almost absent from the school's history, for example, with only a handful of fights occurring between students since Garza's opening in 1998. As stated previously, this may be because Garza teachers and staff create an environment where a lot of concerns and insecurities are addressed and destigmatized. Students often report feeling accepted within the school by both their teachers and their peers. Garza has found ways to decease interpersonal conflicts by normalizing and destigmatizing difficult topics and using SFBT to communicate and mediate issues between peers and between students and teachers. The school also emphasizes restitution and learning instead of punishment, and this responsibility is also put in the hands of the students. When students are given detention, for example, they are required not only to think about what they did that got them into trouble but also to explore what they could have done differently. They are asked to envision what a solution would look like and how they can make those changes. The following quote from Sam Watson, former assistant principal, shows the positive results:

> During detention, students are given a thought sheet that is used to help [them] write out what happened. We would ask specific questions like what happened the first time, what happened the second time, what could you have done to keep that from happening, what will you do the next time this happens? And so that was a way for us not to have to sit there with them but still engaged them in some mental reflection about what happened. So it became, what can we do to do a better job? What could you have done for this not to happen? What were some of the other choices you could have made? What can you do to correct that? So the kids would rattle off solutions to those questions for you because they know the right answers.

Implementing SFBT in the Alternative School

Solution-focused strategies were not forced upon the campus staff overnight; rather, the process was gradual and self-motivated. Undoubtedly, the administration's engagement is critical to the success of Garza as an alterative high school. Garza opened its doors in 1998, and the training toward SFBT started in 2001. The school was well prepared to accept the SFBT training, however, and already had multiple factors that contributed to its success as an alternative school, having purposefully adopted the best practices it could find in alternative school education. These factors, referred to as "school readiness factors," that assisted Garza include a constructive organization culture, a horizontal power structure in which all staff and teachers are perceived as capable of making a valuable contribution to the school, staff flexibility to take risks and receive constructive feedback, as well as monetary support and staff to continue the ongoing training and supervision in SFBT (Franklin & Hopson, 2007).

Different schools will of course have different levels of school readiness. The following are suggested steps for determining the readiness of a school and helping the school move toward use of SFBT:

1. Determine the overall willingness and motivation of a school to learn the solution-focused model. Obtain commitment from the administration, and guide administrators to sell the approach to

interested staff who will participate in the learning on a team instead of mandating the training.

2. Motivate a team of individuals that includes members of important constituents (e.g., principal, teachers, counselors, and social workers) to learn a new way of working with students. This is more than a quick training and going through the motions. Time commitments must be blocked out on the school schedule, and the training must be included in professional development. It is recommended that a training timeline and set of goals be developed with the principal and team who will be participating.

3. Create specific learning steps in the training process. This should be planned out with the team across an entire academic year. For example, first teach the philosophy of SFBT and the specific techniques in a series of small groups and meetings. Second, build in the steps to facilitate the learning of others and the application of techniques in the classroom. Third, provide specific methods to coach and provide feedback on the learning. Fourth, facilitate an ongoing follow-up process to discuss the applications.

4. Continue training the original team in smaller group meetings, and provide them with opportunities to be partners in teaching others the approach.

As stated previously, every staff member on campus should become extremely fluent in SFBT. Professional development and staff leadership are essential to the success of Tier 1 interventions and integral to the building of a solution-focused school. There is also a process to becoming a solution-focused school. The focus is not on immediate change but, rather, on small steps and measurable goals that a campus can make to become solution focused. The leadership team and teachers set these goals and define the small steps they will take. The steps below relate to the staff-training component of becoming solution focused. These ideas for how to improve their own competencies in the approach were designed and implemented by the faculty and staff at Garza during its transition from a beginning alternative school program to a solution-focused program.

1. A library of solution-focused resources were made available to the teachers and other staff.

2. Teachers organized themselves into groups and formed a book club for readings.
3. Brown-bag lunch meetings were scheduled for teachers, staff, and administrators to watch and discuss videos of solution-focused interventions.
4. In-service trainings for the entire staff were organized with an SFBT trainer. This trainer also met with smaller groups (e.g., the principal, administrators, and counselors) for additional training and consultation. Throughout the school's training process, other solution-focused trainers were brought in to inspire and boost the learning sessions.
5. A solution-focused coach worked within the school and was available for classroom consultations and modeling of the solution-focused approach. This involved periodic visits to the classroom. The solution-focused trainers observed teachers leading classroom groups and using techniques like the miracle question and also provided written, complimentary feedback about a teacher's use of the SFBT.
6. Teachers were provided with quick reference sheets for solution-focused techniques they could use with students. Follow-up meetings invited discussions about how the techniques were used so that teachers were teaching other teachers how to use the SFBT techniques.
7. The administration added competencies in solution-focused intervention to the annual performance evaluation with faculty and staff.

Schoolwide Examples of the SFBT Principles

A Tier 1 approach indicates that the solution-focused philosophy needs to guide interpersonal interactions and direct campuswide events so that these events are built on principles such as focusing on strengths, relationships, and community building. Garza High School instituted Mix-It-Up Days, for example, which are community events held every semester that include: inspirational speakers; student talent shows; student, faculty and community lunches; and a host of community visitors known as "friends of Garza" who offer unique and caring contributions to the school. In addition to the regular graduation ceremony, Garza also has a Star Walk. Since Garza's curriculum is self-paced, students often graduate in the middle of the semester. When a student completes all of the necessary credits, the entire school participates in each student's individual Star Walk. Box 4.2 describes a Star Walk in the 2015–2016 school year.

Box 4.2 Star Walk

Three years ago, Martín thought he would never graduate high school. He had been struggling academically at his previous high school and had poor attendance. After enrolling in Garza High School, Martín started taking classes such as robotics and filmmaking. Martín never thought of himself as a good student, but these classes captured his attention more than those at his previous school. Martín became invested in his work at Garza when his mom lost her job. Since Martín's mom was out of work, he had to take a day job. This meant that Martín had to leave school at lunch to work. Luckily, Martín's teachers were supportive of his unusual schedule and helped him finish his coursework over the next two years.

Now, Martin has completed his high school and begun his Star Walk. First, Martin presented some of his work to his teachers as well as his mother. Martín's presentation focused on the work he had done in this filmmaking class. At this presentation, Martín received positive feedback as a teacher read a letter of reference aloud. Next, Martín was presented with an inscribed star emblem. A photograph was taken of Martín and his counselor while the administration listed some of Martín's future goals, such as enrolling in college to learn more about filmmaking. Finally, Martín took a last walk through the halls of Garza. Martín asked his mom and his counselor to walk with him. As the trio strolled through the school, celebratory music played over the intercom speakers. Students and teachers flooded out of classrooms to celebrate Martín's success. Some of his peers blew bubbles, some clapped, and others brought out instruments to play. Although Martín had celebrated the Star Walk of previous students, he had not imagined his own. To Martín, this ritual felt like a rite of passage. Now that he had been successful at Garza, Martín felt that he could be successful in other places. He had set goals for himself in high school and, with the support of staff and teachers at Garza, had met them.

The Star Walk is one of the more prevalent campuswide solution-focused initiatives at Garza. It aligns with the process of SFBT as it reinforces the student's ability to meet self-set goals, and it highlights strengths and competence and allows the student to receive compliments about success. This ritual celebrates the student's individuality and self-motivation. In the case example of Box 4.2, we can see the entire Garza community celebrate the success of the student by pointing out his competencies and goals. The administration also takes time to celebrate the student by presenting them with their star paperweight, telling a personal, positive testimonial about the student and taking a picture with the student. Note the unique classes Martín took; these courses allowed him to receive credits for high school but were more engaging than a traditional curriculum. In these classes, Martín explored possible postsecondary interests and learned real-world skills. The unique curriculum at Garza fits into the solution-focused model as it allows teachers to take risks within their teaching plans and capitalizes on students' intrinsic motivation to learn. For schools wanting to incorporate solution-focused techniques into campuswide initiatives, it is essential that the entire school community celebrates the use of solution-focus strategies as well as the student's individual accomplishments (Franklin, Moore, & Hopson, 2008).

Academic Achievement and Success

In 2015, only 4 of the 12 high schools in the AISD met federal standards. One of these high schools was Gonzalo Garza Independence High School. What is surprising about this achievement is that Garza is a high school where most of the students are considered to be at risk by the school district. As an alternative school, Garza has many components that contribute to its overall success, but a unique characteristic discussed in this chapter is that the school adopted SFBT as an integral part of its philosophy and techniques. The developers of the solution-focused school hoped to create a setting that would enable at-risk youth to overcome barriers to academic success and ultimately earn credits and a high school diploma leading to enrollment in postsecondary education. Last year, Garza achieved this success with over 80% of its graduates enrolled into postsecondary education programs by graduation.

To date, five evaluation studies have focused on Garza High School. These include a quasi-experimental design (Franklin, Streeter, Kim, &

Tripodi, 2007), a qualitative design (Lagana-Riordan et al., 2011) and a concept mapping methodology (Streeter, Franklin, Kim, & Tripodi, 2011). A fifth longitudinal study that examine on-time graduation rates of students who participated in the school over a four-year time frame is in progress, but the results of that study are yet not available for dissemination. The other four evaluations are described below.

The first study (Franklin et al., 2007) utilized a quasi-experimental pre-test/posttest comparison groups design. Participants (n = 46) in the experimental group all attended Garza High School (solution-focused alternative school [SFAS]). Because no additional alternative school was available, the comparison group participants (n = 39) were recruited from a traditional local public high school. Comparison group participants were matched with the experimental group using the following characteristics: attendance, number of credits earned, participation in the free lunch program, race, gender, and whether the student was defined as at risk according the Texas Education Code.

Three dependent variables were observed in this study: credits earned, attendance, and graduation rates. Data for these three variables were obtained through the AISD records. The results of this quasi-experimental study offer researchers and practitioners insight toward understanding the potential impact of the solution-focused school on students' school credits earned, attendance, and graduation rates. Repeated-measures analysis of variance revealed no significant difference between the comparison group (matched students attending a regular local public high school dropout prevention program) and the SFAS participants during the 2002–2003 academic school year; however, a significant difference was found between groups during the 2003–2004 academic school year, indicating that students enrolled in the SFAS earned a greater proportion of credits than the students in the comparison group. One important aspect to consider is the pace at which students progress through the SFAS program as compared to that of students in the traditional high school setting. Garza is a self-paced, individualized program that allows students the flexibility to attend school for half days, to work part-time, and for some, to be a parent as well. The results suggested that some students in the SFAS required about one year longer to finish high school than those in a traditional high school. One possible conclusion from this study is that while Garza students may take slightly longer, they also display a greater likelihood of completing credits when they were much further behind compared to the students who participated in another dropout prevention program.

The second study (Lagana-Riordan et al., 2011) employed a qualitative case study methodology and recruited participants from the experimental group in the first study (Franklin et al., 2007). Of the 46 students who were asked to participate, 33 elected to do so. The students were primarily Caucasian (54.6%) or Hispanic (39.9%), and more than half (57.6%) were female. Each participant answered 36 questions in a 45- to 60-minute, semi-structured interview. The interview questions were a combination of scaling questions, list items, and open-ended questions. The interviewers used probes to gather additional information.

The questions and probes coalesced around topics related to satisfaction with current and previous schools, family history, and relationships with peers and family. Responses were transcribed, coded, and theoretically grouped using a thematic analysis. Methods to provide rigor and trustworthiness included triangulations with quantitative data, persistent observation, and prolonged engagement. The thematic analysis results of this qualitative study (Lagana-Riordan et al., 2011) revealed several differences in students' SFAS (Garza High School) and traditional school experiences. The majority of the perceptions students described about the SFAS were positive. Specifically, the major positive themes that emerged were positive teacher relationships, improving maturity level and responsibility, alternative structure, understanding about social issues, and positive peer relationships. Participants in the study explained that the SFAS atmosphere was one where teachers and peers offered understanding, support, and a greater level of individualized attention. Additionally, students described the school's flexibility and expectations of empowering responsibility to be central to their success.

Several themes regarding the students' perceptions of the major weaknesses of traditional schools also emerged: problems with teachers, lack of safety, overly rigid authority, inadequate school structure, and problems with peer relationships. Students expressed feelings of being judged by peers and teachers. Additionally, they felt that traditional schools were not able to offer the individualized attention or safety necessary to foster effective learning. The findings from this study reveal important characteristics for school social workers and other practitioners to consider when intervening in the life of students at risk of school dropout.

The third study (Streeter et al., 2011) utilized a concept mapping design. Concept mapping is a mixed-methods approach to help examine a program's fidelity towards its guiding theory and philosophy and to evaluate the most important program features contributing to the program's mission to graduate at-risk students. Fourteen students and 37 adults (teachers, administrators, and staff) participated in the concept mapping sessions and generated a combined total of 182 unique statements as a response to the following statement: *Describe the specific characteristics of the alternative school that help students achieve their educational goals.* The results of the concept mapping evaluation offered 15 clusters reflecting participants' descriptions and understandings of the alternative school: relationships, professional environment, respect evident throughout the school, strengths based, sense of community, student-student interaction, empowering culture, cutting edge, organizational foundation, school size and structure of the school day, admission and exit, resources directed to student success, preparation for life, student success, and continuous improvement.

These was driven by the pragmatist approach of grounded theory and the constant comparative method described by Glaser and Strauss (2007), and it sought to discover a relevant theory for teacher-student interactions. Data collection stopped when incoming data had reached the point of saturation (Morse, 1995; Timmermans & Tavory, 2012), meaning that the categories could be "fully accounted, [with] the variability between them [being] explained and the relationships between them . . . tested and validated" (O'Reilly & Parker, 2012, pp. 190–197). The final model represented the overarching core category and subthemes from the teacher interviews (Hallberg, 2006) and the researcher revisited individual narratives in the results section to enhance the richness of the data (Ayres, Kavanaugh, & Knafl, 2003; Szlyk, 2016).

Of 58 potential staff members, 10 teachers participated in individual, semistructured interviews, and four teachers participated in a focus group. All teachers were trained in SFBT, in accordance with the school's mission. The teachers had varying years of experience with SFBT but no other mental health experience. Teachers described at-risk behaviors including truancy, substance abuse, suicidal ideation, and self-harm as being the most prevalent problems of their students. Teachers reported being confronted with these issues daily but expressed a confidence and calmness in the way they interacted with the students around their emotional concerns and external threats to the student's well-being. Teachers also described building strong relationships with their students, which served as a foundation for addressing both academic and emotional concerns that arise in the classroom. Results from this study specifically demonstrated how teachers were able to focus on the academic and emotional needs of their students using skilled decision making, thoughtful interactions, and continued awareness of the presenting problems. A core construct was identified to be social responsibility created by the faculty's teaching philosophy, as driven by the SFBT approach, daily student-teacher interactions, and the values of the school itself. The findings of this research suggested that teachers had a great sense of social mission and a caring, committed teaching philosophy that influenced their daily interactions with students. Specifically:

> This teaching philosophy was often one of the reasons that the participants were attracted to the alternative high school. Teachers discussed having a previous desire to "put students' strengths first," "to treat students as if they were [their] own children," and to give students "gifts" to make the world a better place. As one teacher put it, ... I think that part of being a teacher is caring about people in general. I don't think it is a very selfish profession. I think you will be miserable if it's just about you all the time.

> (Szlyk, 2016, p. 13).

The results from the core category of social responsibility suggested that teachers nurtured the growth and independence of their students. Student independence is fostered as a result of collaborative problem solving between the student and teacher during times of crisis or emotional distress. Teachers relied on the SFBT skills to facilitate the collaborative problem-solving process, making it possible for them to help students with the daily setbacks and distress that often occurred in the classroom.

Data Collected by the School District

The AISD and the Texas Education Agency have also collected data on the characteristics and academic achievement of Garza High School. According to the latest data from the Texas Education Agency (2014), 75.9% of Garza students from the class of 2014 were classified as being at risk, but in 2014, 88.7% of students on the four-year graduation plan graduated, received a

GED, or continued enrollment in school. In 2014, Garza had a dropout rate of 4.2% and an attendance rate of 81.6%. That same year, 42.4% of Garza graduates were deemed to be college or employment ready, and the average SAT scores of Garza students were higher than the average SAT scores of the school district and the state of Texas. It is common for Garza's students and staff to be recognized at a district, state, or national level for their efforts and successes. In February 2016, Garza's chess team took first place at regional competition, with several students on the team taking home individual awards. In the 2013–2014 school year, Garza received exemplary ratings in every category of the 2013–2014 Campus Community & Student Engagement Ratings. Additionally, in 2015, Dr. Linda Webb received the Principal of the Year Award from the AISD. Two other staff members have been recently recognized: one of the counselors as a Counselor That Change Lives for 2015, and a social studies teacher featured on the district website for Garza's blended curriculum.

Start Your Own Solution-Focused School

Garza High School serves as a model program for how a public, alternative school makes the shift to a strengths-based school that uses the behavioral change procedures offered by SFBT. By using the solution-focused approach, Garza became a place that provides emotional support, social support and engages students who receive limited support from family, friends, and neighborhood. This type of social support and individualized attention appears to be critical for retention and graduation of some at-risk students. Research indicates that family problems, mental health, and substance use issues are associated with high school dropouts (Aloise-Young & Chavez, 2002; Nowicki, Duke, Sisney, Stricker, & Tyler, 2004; Rumberger & Thomas, 2000), and this is the daily experience of school social workers and teachers working with students at Garza High School. Other schools may also experience the greatest severity of these types of problems because of the developmental issues confronting adolescence and the worsening over time of trauma and unresolved problems. Without strategies to assist students with complex behavioral health issues, it is unlikely that schools will be able to successfully graduate every student. SFBT is an approach that school social workers can use to train all staff in schools to help at-risk students with severe social and behavioral health problems. In particular, teachers can be equipped in the philosophy and techniques of SFBT and adapt it for use in their classrooms. That Garza High School has maintained the solution-focused approach for 15 years also suggests that teachers and school staff not only can be trained in this approach but that the SFBT approach has the potential to sustain itself over time. This, coupled with the fact that the school is successful at graduating and sending high-risk students to postsecondary education, indicates that SFBT will be worth the investment for a school district to create an SFBT program.

Summary

This chapter opened by briefly describing an RtI and Tier 1 approach to interventions and how SFBT can be used to create a Tier 1 intervention for dropout prevention. A transdisciplinary team model to train educators in SFBT was also described. With the use of case examples, the chapter next described how SFBT techniques were utilized in Tier 1 interventions within Gonzalo Garza Independence High School, a solution-focused, alternative high school in Austin, Texas. The techniques and case examples exemplified challenges commonly observed in at-risk students with behavioral health challenges such as suicidal ideation, self-harm, violence, and aggression. The examples also demonstrated school-based mental health services and discipline and how the Garza staff operate as a team. The school's principal, Dr. Linda Webb, notes that "Garza takes a collaborative approach to finding solutions." This is why staff members are trained in solution-focused techniques, including identifying strengths, looking for small and measurable solutions, and seeking exceptions to the problem. These skills can be used, in most situations, by the entire staff, who undergo extensive training in the application of these methods. After receiving such training, it is possible for all school staff surrounding the students to be involved in their goals and their successes. This campuswide involvement and investment, achieved through SFBT, is a central part of a successful Tier 1 intervention.

Both evaluation research on Garza High School and data collected from the school district provide evidence for the positive academic achievement and success of Garza. Garza has maintained high achievement and graduation success despite over 75% of the students being considered at risk. The school, its staff, and its students also have won numerous awards. Students are active in their education, participating in various districtwide events and creating useful projects in their classes that continue being used after their graduation. Examples of these projects can be viewed on Garza's website (http://garzaindependencehs.weebly.com). This solution-focused, student-faculty engagement continues after high school as many students enroll in a university (Garza raises substantial scholarship funds to support the students' postsecondary goals) or become employed. It is feasible for school social workers to assist school districts in learning from the success of Garza and developing their own SFAS that may improve their graduation and postsecondary enrollment of at-risk students.

References

Allen-Meares, P., Montgomery, K. L., & Kim, J. S. (2013). School-based social work interventions: A cross-national systematic review. *Social Work, 58*(3), 253–262.

Aloise-Young, P. A., & Chavez, E. L. (2002). Not all school dropouts are the same: Ethnic differences in the relation between reason for leaving school and adolescent substance use. *Psychology in the Schools, 39*(5), 539–547.

Ayres, L., Kavanaugh, K., & Knafl, K. A. (2003). Within-case and across-case approaches to qualitative data analysis. *Qualitative Health Research, 13*(6), 871–883.

Franklin, C., & Hopson L. M. (2007). Facilitating the use of evidence-based practices in community organizations. *The Journal of Social Work Education, 43*(3), 377–404. doi:10.5175/JSWE.2007.200600027

Franklin, C., Kim, J.S., Ryan, T. N., Kelly, M. S., & Montgomery, K. (2012). Teacher involvement in mental health interventions: A systematic review. *Children & Youth Services Review, 34*, 973–982. doi:10.1016/j.childyouth.2012.01.027

Franklin, C., Montgomery, K., Baldwin, V., & Webb, L. (2012). Research and development of a solution-focused high school. In C. Franklin, T. Trepper, W. Gingerich, & E. McCollum (Eds.), *Solution-focused brief therapy: A handbook of evidence-based practice* (pp. 371–389). New York, NY: Oxford University Press.

Franklin, C., Moore, K., & Hopson, L. (2008). Effectiveness of solution-focused brief therapy in a school setting. *Children & Schools, 30*(1), 15–26.

Franklin, C., & Streeter, C. L. (2004). *Solution-focused accountability schools for the 21st century.* Austin, TX: The Hogg Foundation for Mental Health, The University of Texas at Austin.

Franklin, C, Streeter, C. L., Kim, J. S., & Tripodi, S. J. (2007). The effectiveness of a solution focused, public alternative school for dropout prevention and retrieval. *Children and Schools, 29*, 133–144.

Glaser, B. G., & Strauss, A. L. (2007). *The discovery of grounded theory: Strategies for qualitative research.* New Brunswick, NJ: Aldine Transaction.

Hallberg, L. R. (2006). The "core category" of grounded theory: Making constant comparisons. *International Journal of Qualitative Studies on Health and Well-being, 1*(3), 141–148.

Jones, C. N., Hart, S. R., Jimerson, S. R., Dowdy, E., Earhart, Jr., J., Renshaw, T. L., & Anderson, D. (2009). Solution-focused brief counseling: Guidelines, considerations, and implications for school psychologists. *The California School Psychologist, 14*(1), 111–122.

Kim, J. S., & Franklin, C. (2009). Solution-focused, brief therapy in schools: A review of the outcome literature. *Children and Youth Services Review, 31*, 461–470.

Lagana-Riordan, C., Aguilar, J. P., Franklin, C., Streeter, C. L., Kim, J. S., Tripodi, S. J., & Hopson, L. M. (2011). At-risk students' perceptions of traditional schools and a solution-focused public alternative school. *Preventing School Failure, 55*(3), 105–114.

Morse, J. M. (1995). The significance of saturation. *Qualitative Health Research, 5*(2), 147–149.

Newsome, W. S. (2005). The impact of solution-focused brief therapy with at-risk junior high school students. *Children & Schools, 27*(2), 83–90.

Nowicki, S., Duke, M. P., Sisney, S., Stricker, B., & Tyler, M. A. (2004). Reducing the drop-out rates of at-risk high school students: The effective learning program (ELP). *Genetic, Social, and General Psychology Monographs, 130*(3), 225–240.

O'Reilly, M., & Parker, N. (2012). "Unsatisfactory Saturation": A critical exploration of the notion of saturated sample sizes in qualitative research. *Qualitative Research, 13*(2), 190–197. doi:10.1177/1468794112446106.

Rumberger, R. W., & Thomas, S. L. (2000). The distribution of dropout and turnover rates among urban and suburban high schools. *Sociology of Education, 73*, 39–67.

Sabatino, C. A., Kelly, E. C., Moriarity, J., & Lean, E. (2013). Response to intervention: A guide to scientifically based research for school social work services. *Children & Schools, 35*(4), 213–223.

Streeter, C. L., & Franklin, C. (2002). Standards for school social work in the 21st century. *Social workers' desk reference*, 612-618.

Streeter, C. L., Franklin, C., Kim, J. S., & Tripodi, S. J. (2011). Concept mapping: An approach for evaluating a public alternative school program. *Children & Schools, 33*(4), 197–214.

Texas Education Agency. (2014). Texas Education Agency 2014. Accountability Summer. Retrieved from: https://rptsvrl.tea.texas.gov/perfreport/account/2014/static/summary/campus/c227901015.pdf

Timmermans, S., & Tavory, I. (2012). Theory construction in qualitative research: From grounded theory to abductive analysis. *Sociological Theory, 30*(3), 167–186.

Szlyk, H. (under review). How do teachers engage at-risk students in the classroom: A grounded theory. Manuscript submitted for publication.

5

SFBT Within the Tier 2 Framework

Coaching Teachers to See the Solutions in Their Classrooms

Michael S. Kelly, Johnny S. Kim, & Cynthia Franklin

Educational research on student behavior and classroom achievement increasingly shows that creative, engaged teachers are able to manage classrooms more effectively than burnt-out teachers or teachers who feel overwhelming pressure to teach to tests (Evertson et al., 2006; Responsive Classroom, 2006). The WOWW program ("Working on What Works") strives to empower teachers in regular and special education settings to recognize their own strength as well as those of their students in setting goals and developing a shared focus as learners. It was first developed by SFBT pioneers Insoo Kim Berg and Lee Shilts in Florida in 2002 (Berg & Shilts, 2004). After being piloted in urban schools in Fort Lauderdale, Florida, the program has been implemented in other cities, including several schools we have worked with in Chicago (Berg & Shilts, 2004; Kelly & Bluestone-Miller, 2009) and several school contexts within and other parts of the United States and the United Kingdom. In this chapter, we share some of our own preliminary findings on WOWW's success in helping students and teachers along with other pilot data on WOWW.

Looking for Solutions in the Teachers' Lounge

One of the toughest places to sit as a school social worker can be the teachers' lounge. A story from Michael Kelly illustrates this:

> I got my pasta out of the microwave and sat down with some teacher colleagues one day before a holiday break. Before I could

take my first bite, one teacher colleague grilled me about what I thought about her class. "You work with half of them in your office, aren't they wild?" asked Betty. "Jeannie (her second-grade teacher colleague) told me that these third graders were going to be hell on wheels for me, and she was right! And the worst two are Sal and Carlos; oh, why did I have to get those two?" Outwardly, I was speechless, as I could tell Betty was just getting started. Inside, I was thinking that it might be time for me to offer more to Betty and her class than just pulling out the kids in her class who had social work services on their individualized education plans.

Soon, other teachers at the table joined in with their stories of Sal and Carlos, one sharing that she works lunch duty on Fridays and thinks that Sal "shouldn't be out at lunch until he can get himself together." Another told a story about how Carlos' dad dropped him off at school, and she heard from another mom that she smelled alcohol on his breath. "There you go, that's what I have to deal with," Betty said, and turned back to me. "So what do you think?"

I took a deep breath, agreed with her that the kids in her class were tough, and told her that I was interested in trying this new program in her class. It was called WOWW, and I thought it might be a good way for me to help get her class under control. She said she'd think about it but quickly added, "But you make sure that the principal knows that she better be ready for me to start sending Sal and Carlos down to her if things don't change soon!"

The negative energy in the teacher's lounge can be thick, as good-natured venting and laughing about job stress can give way to colleagues turning to you and asking questions about the kids you work with ("What's *wrong* with Billy, anyway?") or offering not-so-professional takes on what makes it hard for some kids at school ("Those Smith boys are all the same. I taught their dad, too, and he was just as crazy"). Being in these situations pushes many of our professional and ethical buttons as we struggle to figure out how to respond (and finish our lunch as well). Although we're still not fans of kicking back in the lounge and gossiping about kids, we have, through SFBT coaching interventions like WOWW, learned to see our teacher colleagues more sympathetically as they grapple with the many demands on their time and the complicated nature of the kids who come through their door each day.

Teachers Are People, Too

It is tempting (and even easy) to see the story of the teacher's lounge as evidence that teachers are perhaps as crazy as the kids they call crazy. It is also tempting to view the role of the school social worker as one where you work with the primary client in most referral situations—the student—in an environment that you largely control (i.e., your own office) and leave the behavioral acting-out and general craziness that occur in the classroom for teachers, principals, and disciplinarians to handle. After all, most of us in the schools are in no obvious position to supervise, discipline, or correct behaviors exhibited in classrooms. Most of us would not want the dual role of disciplining the very students we are also trying to counsel, either, but what about our feelings toward our teaching colleagues? How many of us have had "those" classrooms, where we know that kids are likely to be yelled at and have their particular social/emotional needs ignored or minimized? Wouldn't it be satisfying if we could just stop the restrictive behavior of these teachers and see whether the kids respond any differently?

Teachers are not monsters, not any more than the kids are. Teachers enter schools excited to give their students a love for learning and to be a person students can look up to. Again and again, teachers fresh to the field report a "love of children" and "a passion for teaching" as part of their reasons for choosing the profession (Kelly & Northrup, 2015; Roehrig, Presley, & Talotta, 2002). Yet research also shows that as many as 50% of those same excited, idealistic teachers will leave the profession altogether after 5 years (Burke, Aubusson, Schuck, Buchanan, & Prescott, 2015; National Education Association, 2007) and this turnover has negative consequences for student achievement, particularly for students in low-income communities (Ronfeldt, Loeb, & Wyckoff, 2013). Something is happening in those initial years to bring so many teachers to the same conclusion that teaching is not for them. What can we learn from the research on teacher retention and burnout?

First and foremost, we would do well to think of all our teacher colleagues in the same way we might think of our clients: as complicated and interesting individuals who bring a multitude of strengths and challenges to their work. In short, teachers are human, and if anything, by doing an SFBT-based intervention like WOWW with them, we help more of that humanity to emerge in their teaching practice while also giving them a chance to share the stresses of the classroom in appropriate, solution-focused ways with the WOWW coach and the students.

Just as we are largely not occupying disciplinary roles in schools, we are usually not involved in supervising and evaluating teacher performance (Constable, 2006). This could be viewed as a burden (having to put up with teachers and a school environment that at times seems hostile to kids), or it could present its own SFBT opportunity. We offer the WOWW program as one way to aid multiple levels of the school contextual system: helping teachers to see their own strengths, students to work together more effectively as a group, and both teachers and students to learn how to be more respectful and accountable to each other in ways that preserve the ultimate authority of the teacher while also empowering students to speak out and act intentionally in positive ways.

The History

As Berg and Shilts (2005) recount, the idea for WOWW came from Shilts' wife, Margaret, sharing her concerns about some of the students she was teaching and the different challenges they presented as she tried to manage the classroom and cover the curriculum. After starting in Florida, the program has been piloted in other states, including several schools we have worked with in Chicago. Later in this chapter, we share some of our own preliminary findings on WOWW's success in helping students and teachers as well as other pilot data on WOWW.

The Skills

WOWW is a coaching intervention, meaning that the solution-focused practitioner operates primarily in a consultative role with the teacher and the classroom. The WOWW coach will both observe the classroom and facilitate group discussions, but the coach never really leads a group intervention in the way that many other group treatment approaches do—that is, the coach is not delivering a specific therapeutic intervention in a specific sequence. Right away, in WOWW, the basic tenets of SFBT are revealed in contrast to other more manualized approaches: the clients (in this case, the teacher and the teacher's students) are put squarely in charge of setting the goals for the WOWW class discussions. Just like in other SFBT interventions, the initial session is full of questions, which are organized around asking the students to notice changes that have already taken place in their class. The difference from a more conventional SFBT clinical session is that the WOWW coach has already observed the class and is able to share observations directly in the form of compliments, exception questions, and coping questions. This aids the eventual final task of the first WOWW session, the setting of classroom goals that relate to the learning environment. Box 5.1 shows examples of learning goals in our WOWW sessions.

The WOWW coach (in our work, usually the school social worker) observes the class functioning for a 20- to 30-minute period and later offers compliments and questions rooted in the SFBT framework. The class is invited to recognize their own strengths and devise solutions to class discipline problems together, rather than singling out a few defiant students. One of the major goals of WOWW coaching is to remove the tendency for classrooms with "a few" difficult students to lose cohesion and a sense of mutual purpose. By bringing the conversation back to what the whole class sees as things they want to change, the effort is made to reach out to more challenging students as well as validate students who are already following the teacher's rules and working well with others.

The following conversation is typical of a WOWW classroom discussion after the coach has observed and worked with the class for a few sessions. This case example comes from our work with a third-grade classroom:

> **School Social Worker (SSW):** Hi, everyone, my name is Mr. Kelly, and I'm going to be coming to your class every week for the next couple of months. I wanted to start by getting a show of hands from all the kids here that can count to 10. Everybody? Good. Now, who knows what the word "perfect" means?
>
> **Student 1:** It means really, really good. So good that you can't do any better.
>
> **SSW:** Good, that's it. What I want us to think about for a minute is our class here. Is this class perfect?
>
> **Students:** No! [laughter]
>
> **SSW:** That's fine; no class I've visited is perfect. But what would you say the class' behavior has been in the past week, on a scale from 1 to 10, with 10 being perfect?

At this point, the SSW had students write down their score and pass them up anonymously, and the SSW and the classroom teacher then tabulated the results. During this time, the SSW was noticing strengths in the

Box 5.1 Phases for the WOWW Coaching Process

WOWW Program Phase	Details
Phase 1: Observation phase (Weeks 1–3 for an hour)	Introduce yourself to students, saying "I'm going to be visiting your classroom to watch for all the things the class does that are good and helpful. I will report back to you what I see."
	Note class strengths, and wait for the class to begin pointing out their own strengths to you, indicating their readiness for the next phase.
	Share what you saw, and prepare the class for creating classroom goals.
Phase 2: Creating classroom goals with students and teachers (Week 4 or 5)	With the teacher and the class, set goals for the class to work toward (e.g., show respect to each others), and ask them to scale the level of respect they have at present on a scale from 1 to 10.
	Ask the class to describe what it will take for the class to go from a 7 to an 8 or a 9, and ask the class to look for those behaviors in themselves and others over the next week.
	Scale other goals that the class is interested in working on.
Phase 3: Scaling classroom success and amplifying (remainder of sessions)	Once the scaling questions are understood, teachers may put the scaling goal on the board as a reminder, and the class will be more focused on reaching the goals set for each week. Amplify the class' progress on their goals, and repeat as needed.

Source: Adapted from Berg and Shilts (2005).

class' behavior and asking for exceptions to the major behavior problems the teacher has identified, mostly related to how the class behaves after lunch. Continuing our case example:

> **SSW:** Thanks for voting: the class average was a 6.5, definitely not perfect, but pretty good. What do you think your class would be doing if next week your votes were an 8? What would be different and better about the behavior in this class?
>
> **Student 2:** We would line up better and be able to sit in our seats after lunch more.
>
> **SSW:** Okay, what else?
>
> **Student 3:** We would listen to our teacher the first time she says something and not make her have to raise her voice after lunch so much. [class laughs, including the teacher]
>
> **SSW:** Great, what else would you need to do?
>
> **Student 4:** Be nicer to each other; we yell a lot in this class sometimes after lunch.

At this point, many of the questions and approaches in the WOWW program will be familiar. As the earlier example shows, WOWW coaches are keen on asking students first to honestly assess their classroom on a particular issue (e.g., how well they listen or how well they line up) and then give themselves a scaled rating between 1 and 10. The next step the WOWW coach takes is to ask more questions from the scaling sequence to help the classroom move toward setting a goal for future classroom sessions. In the case example, students said they were at about a 6.5 in terms of their listening to the teacher after lunch. This seemingly small part of the day was actually a huge destabilizer for the afternoon, as many students failed to get on track and others said they wished that the teacher didn't have to yell so much to get the class settled. Improving this part of the day was identified by both teachers and students as a key area to focus on, and by asking scaling questions, the WOWW coach was able to assess how much progress the class thought was realistic for the coming week.

In addition to the importance placed on getting students to mobilize around their inherent strengths, ample attention is paid to what the teacher hopes to change about the classroom. In class discussions as well as debriefings with the WOWW coach after school, teachers are invited to share their perceptions of the students' behavior and their goals for change. Unlike other classroom management models that try gimmicks or external rewards, the WOWW coaching intervention is interested in teachers and students discovering what small gains they are making and then "doing more of what's working" to turn those successes into larger gains for the whole classroom environment.

The teacher debriefing times are crucial to maximize the impact of the WOWW program. In these confidential sessions, the teacher is given the same opportunities as the students to reflect on the classroom and identify his or her own capacities and strengths. Here is an example of a WOWW coach debriefing, from the same third-grade classroom discussed earlier:

SSW: Thanks for meeting with me today. How's the day been?

Mrs. Smith (MS): Really good; the kids have been great. It's one of those days where you keep wondering when the other shoe's going to drop when they get back from lunch. It's almost too perfect . . .

SSW: Those kinds of days are amazing, but also a little nerve-wracking. Have you noticed anything you were doing differently this morning to help the kids be so well behaved?

MS: No, I can't think . . . well, I did wind up singing to them this morning.

SSW: Wait, you . . . sang?

MS: Yeah, today the principal made an announcement about the class song contest for the spirit day, and I was telling the class about my favorite song, "Dancing Queen" by ABBA. The kids said they'd never heard of it, and I told them that they needed to hear it before they got to fourth grade. Billy dared me to sing it, so I did. The kids just fell out laughing, and then they gave me a standing ovation.

SSW: You just sang, just like that?

MS: I did; I've never done that before. I mean, I like to sing with my family and at church, but I don't think the kids ever heard me sing before.

SSW: That's awesome. What makes you think that might have affected their behavior today?

MS: I'm not sure. Maybe because the kids were having fun, and it was only 8:15 in the morning! Or maybe they were able to see that I was in a good mood and that they could relax with me today.

SSW: What do you mean by "relaxing with you"? Are there times when you're more relaxed that you notice you get a different response from the kids?

MS: Totally. The kids totally take their cue from me; if I'm loose and having fun, we all do better together.

The Research

Developed in 2004, WOWW uses the components of SFBT to facilitate positive interactions in the classroom between teachers and students. The mental health practitioner serves in a consultative role with the teacher and the classroom. Initial pilot studies indicate that WOWW has the potential to impact teachers' sense of self-efficacy and their capacity to avoid burnout. In terms of student outcomes, some promising initial data support the intervention's ability to increase student attendance and engagement in learning. To date, results of five pilot studies based on the current version of WOWW have been published.

The first study (Kelly, Liscio, Bluestone-Miller, & Shilts, 2011) was conducted by one of WOWW's creators (Shilts) and a doctoral student (Liscio) and looked at increasing attendance, improving student behavior, and improving teacher classroom management behavior in 12 special education, middle school classrooms in Florida. Data were collected from 105 students in the WOWW group (based on their teachers volunteering to be in the treatment group) and 101 students from six classrooms that were selected to serve as the comparison group. The generalized estimating equation model was used to test differences between groups on grades, absences, tardiness, school suspensions, and state academic test scores. Results showed statistically significant differences favoring WOWW on decreasing excused absences and tardiness but significant differences favoring the comparison group on unexcused absences. No differences between groups were found on grades, state academic test scores, and school suspensions.

A second WOWW pilot study (Kelly & Bluestone-Miller, 2009) was conducted in 20 urban elementary school classrooms in Illinois and aimed to improve class behavior and teacher self-efficacy. A pretest-posttest design was used with a convenience sample of 21 teachers to examine their perceived classroom management skills as well as how they perceived their students' behavior. The researchers developed a five-point scale for the participating teachers and analyzed data using repeated-measures t-tests to examine differences. Results showed a statistically significant increase in teachers' perceptions of their class as better behaved [$t(20) = 2.6$, $p < .01$], increase in teachers' view of students as better behaved [$t(20) = 3.2$, $p < .05$] and belief students would also report better behavior [$t(20) = 2.8$, $p < .05$], and increase in teachers' positive perceptions of their classroom management skills [$t(20) = 1.9$, $p < .05$]. While these results show promise in improving teacher's classroom management, the lack of a comparison group, small sample size, strong social desirability effects due to teachers not being masked to the intervention, lack of validated measures, and lack of student reports limit the ability of this study to show causality from the WOWW intervention.

A recent WOWW pilot study in Massachusetts (Berzin, O'Brien, & Tohn, 2012) involved second-grade classrooms in a suburban school district using a cohort control design with pre- and posttests. All interested classrooms were eligible to participate, with a final sample of nine teachers and 200 students agreeing to receive the WOWW intervention. Student data on academic performance (e.g., report cards) and behavior (e.g., office referral and guidance counselor visits) were collected for the WOWW group and compared with the previous year's administrative outcomes for second graders. Data on teachers were collected using a series of subscales from the Teacher's Sense of Efficacy Scale, Teacher Stress Inventory, and Student-Teacher Relationship Scale. Positive postintervention trends were found on teacher efficacy questions related to motivating students, establishing a classroom management system, and adjusting lessons. However, no postintervention differences were found on teachers' stress or teacher-student relationships. Results also showed the ability for students in the WOWW program to improve their on-task behavior and increase their academic effort based on district report card data, but no differences were found in behavioral outcomes. Despite the limitations of the study (e.g., no direct comparison group, no random assignment at the classroom level, and limited comparison data), positive trends were found around improving classroom dynamics and student outcomes.

Additionally, WOWW has made some impact in the United Kingdom, where at least two studies of WOWW in elementary-age classrooms have been conducted during the past few years (Brown, Powell, & Clark, 2012; Fernie & Chebbedu, 2016). These studies have continued to show promise for WOWW as a teacher coaching intervention, with both finding that the classroom behavioral and social-emotional goals set by the teachers and students together were met and maintained at follow-up.

Although these early findings show promise for the intervention, some of the mixed results across the different sample sites suggest more work is needed in refining the intervention protocol and evaluating WOWW using a more systematic research design. The studies noted above have been pilots in nature and thus have not been rigorous enough to collect fidelity and process data that could demonstrate the promise of the intervention as well as be used to improve the intervention protocol. Additionally, more evidence is needed about the potential multiple school contexts in which this intervention could be used successfully.

The Future

WOWW has an intuitive appeal to school social workers trying to find positive and non-threatening ways to help teachers and students function better together in a classroom setting. It is a promising new idea that is trying to use the active ingredients of SFBT to make meaningful impacts on classroom behavior, teacher resilience, and student achievement. Currently, it is far too early to say whether WOWW can positively impact such important variables in schools. We hope to bring the WOWW program to more classrooms in Chicago and the surrounding suburbs and study the program in those settings, with larger sample sizes and classes acting as control groups.

One major issue that has already become clear is how best to "sell" this program to schools. The initial WOWW program in Florida was explicit about being completely voluntary in terms of teacher participation, and we followed that same idea in our recruitment of the seven teachers who participated in our pilot study (Kelly & Bluestone-Miller, 2009). In two of our three schools, however, the principals clearly were eager to expand the WOWW program by requiring that all teachers participate, particularly the ones the principal thought might be burned out or even at risk of being fired. This caused challenges for our research team. We wanted to respect the wishes of the principal while avoiding the possibility that WOWW would become yet another thing forced onto teachers' already busy plates. Eventually, we were able to avoid a conflict with the principal by agreeing to do a larger version of the WOWW program in a future year and, at that time, consider the principal's wishes that the program be expanded to cover more troubled teachers. An obvious concern we had was that WOWW not be seen as an extension of the school's teacher evaluation program and the WOWW coach be somehow viewed as a "spy" for the principal and administrative team.

Future larger-scale implementations and evaluation of the WOWW program will have to contend with these issues. Teachers are likely to view any mandatory classroom management program with suspicion, and principals are likely to want the results of the WOWW program to be available to them. This has been a problem with other teacher classroom management training programs (Marzano, 2003), and as we study WOWW on a larger scale, we expect to contend with these implementation challenges for a while to come.

Summary

Savvy school social workers have long known that one of the primary client populations in schools is their teacher colleagues. The WOWW program is a teacher coaching intervention that helps school social workers target their interventions at a classroom level with the teacher and classroom as the "client." This intervention has shown some initial positive outcomes in pilot studies, and in the coming years, we hope to see larger-scale studies on WOWW's impacts on teacher classroom management styles, teacher burnout, and student variables like academic achievement and attendance. With the ever-increasing pressure on both teachers and students to be productive, we believe that school social workers need to use classroom interventions such as WOWW to identify the strengths of classrooms and help both teachers and students work together more effectively.

References

Berg, I., & Shilts, L. (2005). *Classroom solutions: WOWW coaching*. Milwaukee, WI: BFTC Press.

Berzin, S., O'Brien, K., & Tohn, S. (2012). Working on what works: A new model for collaboration. *School Social Work Journal, 36*(2), 15–26.

Brown, E. L., Powell, E., & Clark, A. (2012). Working on what works: Working with teachers to improve classroom behavior and relationships. *Educational Psychology in Practice, 28*(1), 19–30.

Burke, P. F., Aubusson, P. J., Schuck, S. R., Buchanan, J. D., & Prescott, A. E. (2015). How do early career teachers value different types of support? A scale-adjusted latent class choice model. *Teaching and Teacher Education,47*, 241–253.

Constable, R. (2006). *21st century school social work*: Plenary address at the Family and Schools Partnership Program, July 2006.

Evertson, C. M., & Weinstein, C. S. (2006). *Handbook of classroom management: Research, practice, and contemporary issues* (pp. viii, 73–95, 1346 pp). Mahwah, NJ: Lawrence Erlbaum Associates Publishers.

Fernie, L., & Cubeddu, D. (2016). WOWW: A solution orientated approach to enhance classroom relationships and behavior within a Primary three class. *Educational Psychology in Practice, 32*(2), 1–12.

Kelly, M. S., & Bluestone-Miller, R. (2009). Working on What Works (WOWW): Coaching teachers to do more of what's working. *Children & Schools, 31,* 35–38.

Kelly, M. S., Liscio, M., Bluestone-Miller, R., & Shilts, L. (2011). Making classrooms more solution-focused for teachers and students: The WOWW teacher coaching intervention. In Franklin, C. (Ed.), *Solution-focused brief therapy: A handbook of evidence-based practice* (pp. 354–370). New York, NY: Oxford University Press.

Kelly, S., & Northrop, L. (2015). Early career outcomes for the "best and the brightest": Selectivity, satisfaction, and attrition in the Beginning Teacher Longitudinal Survey. *American Educational Research Journal, 52,* 624–656. doi:10.3102/0002831215587352.

Marzano, R. J. (2003). *What works in schools: Translating research into action.* Alexandria, VA: Association for Supervision and Curriculum Development.

National Education Association. (2007). Attracting and keeping quality teachers. Retrieved August 4, 2007, from http://www.nea.org/teachershortage/index.html

Responsive Classroom. (2006). Social and Academic Learning Study (SALS). Retrieved August 1, 2007, from http://www.responsiveclassroom.org/research/index.html

Roehrig, A., Presley, M., & Talotta, D. (2002). *Stories of beginning teachers: First-year challenges and beyond.* South Bend, IN: Notre Dame Press.

Ronfeldt, M., Loeb, S., & Wyckoff, J. (2013). How teacher turnover harms student achievement. *American Educational Research Journal, 50,* 4–36.

6

SFBT Within the Tier 3 Framework
Case Examples of School Social Workers Using SFBT

Michael S. Kelly, Johnny S. Kim, & Cynthia Franklin

This chapter presents a series of case studies showing how school social workers have adapted SFBT to their school contexts. Using a variety of treatment modalities (family, small group, and macro practice), these school social workers show how flexible and powerful SFBT ideas can be in a school setting and how they apply nicely across all three tiers of intervention through the Multi-tiered System of Supports/Response to Intervention framework.

Ultimately, the research on SFBT in schools can only give so much direction, context, and inspiration. Based on the feedback we have received from teaching SFBT ideas, we know that school social workers need and want to hear how others have "done it" and adapted SFBT to their own school social work practices. This chapter offers a series of brief case studies in which school social workers:

1. Used SFBT techniques to change the direction of a case study evaluation meeting to focus more on student and family strengths (Tier 3).
2. Conducted a session of SFBT family therapy led by a school social worker in a school-based mental health clinic (Tier 3).
3. Led SFBT group treatment for students struggling with anxiety (Tier 2 or Tier 3).
4. Mapped out a solution-focused needs assessment that helped a school social worker create a family health and employment fair in an impoverished community (Tier 1).

5. Organized and conducted an eight-week SFBT group session for grandparents raising grandchildren (GRGs), drawing on grandparents' "old-school wisdom" for raising their grandchildren (Tier 2) (Newsome & Kelly, 2004).

Where available, we also provide additional resources for SFBT school social workers on how they can adopt these practice ideas themselves. Key identifying information about the schools have been changed to protect confidentiality, but all of the case examples are based on real practitioners' work and show how SFBT can be incorporated into school social work practice.

A Solution-Focused Case Study Process

School social workers nationwide often participate in case study evaluations (Gleason, 2007; Watkins & Kurtz, 2001) to discern eligibility for special education placement and services. These evaluations are based on diagnostic criteria outlined in the Individuals with Disabilities Education Improvement Act (IDEA) rules and regulations (Altshuler & Kopels, 2003; Constable, 2006) and reflect a deficit model common to diagnostic criteria used in special education (Gleason, 2007; House, 2002). The case example that follows shows how a school social worker used the ideas of resilience and the strengths perspective in SFBT to conduct a routine case study evaluation.

Jenny was practicing in her elementary school for 5 years when she decided to do something different with her special education evaluations. For years, she had been the person to speak after the classroom teacher and the nurse had given their reports and before the school psychologist shared the results of her testing. Most of the reports Jenny gave tried gamely to focus on the student's strengths and capacities for succeeding in both regular and special education, but something always seemed to fall flat. The clinical and family information she was collecting focused primarily on what was not working with the student and his or her family, and though she tried to soften the more diagnostic language inherent in assessing child and family functioning, she wondered whether families heard any of the strengths she was presenting or just words like "deficits" and "disorder" instead. Working as a white school social worker with a majority African American student population, she also worried about the tendency of her special education team to focus on family and student problems rather than on any of the family system's strengths.

After attending some SFBT trainings offered by the Loyola Family and School Partnerships Program, Jenny learned of two rating scales that might help fulfill her report-writing responsibilities but also move the special education eligibility process to one more focused on student capacities and strengths. These two rating scales, the Behavior & Emotional Rating Scale, Second Edition (BERS-2), and the School Success Profile, are contained in the chapter's reference section (Bowen, Rose, & Bowen, 2005; Epstein & Sharma, 2004).

To change her special education assessment process, Jenny started with her own interviews. Using some material from SFBT, she reshaped her student interview and the family social development form to reflect more solution-focused and strength-based ideas (Gleason, 2007; Murphy, 1996). After completing the student interview and receiving the written social developmental study paperwork from each student's parents, she followed up with a phone call to the parents to confirm the information and explore what other information might indicate the student had begun making changes in academic or behavioral performance during the interval between the initial consent for the case study and the case study meeting (pre-session change). Finally, Jenny would ask the parents and the student's classroom teacher to each complete a copy of the BERS-2, and then use these BERS-2 data to help frame the student's difficulties in terms of strengths that he or she had already exhibited and other areas that needed more work or were "emerging." Based on the student's motivation and cognitive levels, she would also often ask the student to complete his or her own student version of the BERS-2, so that she had three sets of strength-oriented data on the student to triangulate and share.

The next all-important step involved fashioning these new data and new perspectives into information that could be shared concisely at the student's special education eligibility meeting. This was no easy task: each meeting was only scheduled for an hour, and there was never any shortage of "problem-talk" to get through regarding why the particular student wasn't behaving appropriately or learning at grade level. Jenny elected to forego her usual read-through of her social history and instead use the BERS-2 data to help her focus on what she saw as the student's strengths and how those strengths might be enhanced to improve the referral problem specified for the case study evaluation.

SFBT Family Therapy

The literature on schools as "community schools" is growing, with attention being paid to helping whole families access services at schools after regular school hours (Anderson-Butcher, Iachini, & Wade-Mdivanian, 2007). Some of those services include after-school tutoring programs, ESL classes for parents, job training programs for teens, and mental health services (Hammond & Reimer, 2006). In the case example that follows, one school social worker who we have worked with describes the family of a student at her school that she saw for a six-session SFBT course of treatment.

> Carol is a school social worker in the large suburban district of Forest Side, outside Chicago. Fifty percent of the students in this district are on the free lunch program; 80% of the district's students are black, 15% are Latino, and 5% are white. Carol has worked in the district for 15 years, and over this period, she has seen minimal improvement in the availability of family-based mental health services in the community, hampering her ability to make solid family therapy referrals for her neediest students. This past year, as part of her professional development goals, she decided to implement an intensive evening family therapy program utilizing SFBT ideas with the students on her caseload who appeared to have significant family struggles. She shared details of one of her cases with us.
>
> Shantel Thomas is a seventh-grade African American who lives with her mother, stepfather, and two younger brothers in Forest Side. Mrs. Thomas (now Mrs. Daniels, after marrying Mr. Daniels 5 years ago and having her two children with him) has lived in Forest Side for all of Shantel's life. Shantel only recently moved back to Forest Side to live full-time with her mother and stepfather, however. For the past 2 years, she had been living with her father and his girlfriend in Chicago, after having run away to her dad's house following a particularly bitter argument with her mother and stepfather. Now she is back at the school social worker's (Carol's) school and is having a number of behavioral and academic adjustments, resulting in several referrals for discipline. Carol observes that Shantel seems to be isolated from other girls in the school's lunchroom. What follows is

the first family session where the school social worker uses scaling questions and the miracle question to mobilize the family around some new solutions for resolving the family's and Shantel's struggles.

School Social Worker (Carol): Hello and welcome back to school! I hope you were able to get to my office with no hassle.

Mr. Daniels (Mr. D): Sure, the school secretary buzzed us in and pointed us up here.

Shantel: And I knew where it was, so I could show them!

Carol: That's great, you could be the tour guide for your parents. Did you show them anything else on your way up here, maybe like where your classroom is?

Shantel: No, I just came here. They can find Ms. Frederick's room on their own time—ooh, I hate her!

Mrs. Daniels (Mrs. D): Shantel! Don't let me hear you talking about your teacher that way. It's only been a month since you started here and already you're talking badly about your teacher. [turning to Carol] See, this is her way. She doesn't given anybody a chance, just makes her mind up and well . . .

Carol: I'm wondering about that, too, Shantel. If you had to say on a scale of 1 to 5, with 1 being not at all comfortable here in your new school and 5 saying that you were totally comfortable here, what would you say your rating is for being at our school?

Shantel: [without hesitation] Oh, a 2, definitely. I mean, it's not like the school totally stinks, but it's nothing like my old school Washington.

Carol: So a 2 is what you would rate our school. What would you have said comfort scale was at Washington?

Shantel: Definitely a 4, maybe even a 5. Yeah, I was real good there.

Mrs. D: You know, she's right about that. My ex-husband told me that Shantel never got any calls home while she was there, and she was even doing . . . what was that club you were in?

Shantel: Wasn't a club, mama. I was in plays and I also did this after-school dance class, too.

Carol: So not only did you rate your school time at Washington higher, you were doing after-school stuff as well?

Shantel: Yeah, it was a great place.

Carol: What would be a way that you could do something at our school to make it feel more like you felt at Washington?

Shantel: Hmm ... I don't know.

Carol: Is there anything that you did at Washington that you think you could "bring" here?

Shantel: I got it. I think I left something at Washington, with my old acting teacher.

Carol: Excuse me?

Shantel: My acting teacher always talked about how we had to hold on to our wisdom while we were doing our parts. He said we all knew more about our characters than the audience did, and we had to hold on to that wisdom and pull it out when we were up there, to make us do a better job.

Carol: That's fascinating. He said you had wisdom, and how old are you?

Shantel: You know how old I am. A lot younger than those two [pointing to mom, everybody laughs].

Mrs. D: Shantel, you are crazy, joking about all this, and we're here to talk about your problems!

Carol: You know, Mrs. Daniels, I think in some ways we are starting to talk about Shantel's problems here at our school. Can I tell you what I've seen happening at school, Shantel?

Shantel: I guess.

Carol: I've talked to your teachers, and they all told me—even Ms. Frederick!—that you are clearly one of the smartest kids in their class. You raise your hand a lot and have good things to contribute. They say that if you did their work, your first-quarter grades would be all A's and B's.

Shantel: Really? I thought they all hated me. They're always looking at me like I did something wrong.

Solution-Focused Brief Therapy in Schools

Mr. D: What about the problems after school and in the lunchroom? I know it's only been a month, but my wife and I have gotten something like five calls from the school asking us to talk to Shantel and to come get her. Getting into fights, back-talking . . . This has got to stop.

Shantel: They're always getting me into trouble! I told you, nobody likes me here! [puts head down, seems ready to either leave the room or cry]

Carol: Shantel, hold on a minute. What your stepdad is saying is true, right, about you getting into some trouble at our school?

Shantel: Yeah, but what else can I do? These other girls are always acting like they own the school or something, tellin' me where to sit, and, oh man, don't get me started on those lunch supervisors . . . they're evil!

Carol: Okay, I think I'm getting a better picture of why you rated our school a 2 for you. I want you to try something with me for a minute. Let's imagine that after we leave here today you go home with your parents, play with your little brothers, do your homework, and then go to sleep.

Shantel: That's pretty much what I would do.

Carol: Great. But this is a different night of going to sleep because while you are sleeping, a miracle happens to you, and when you wake up and come back to school, everything that was a problem for you here is different, all the things that have been bothering you here are different somehow.

Shantel: So . . . like all those mean girls and teachers are gone?

Carol: No, the miracle happens with everybody still at school, including you. What's different is that the problems are gone.

Shantel: Hmm.

Carol: So, my question to you first, and then I'll ask your parents their answer, is "What would you notice first that was different?"

Shantel: [thinks for a long time] I know: I'd have my wisdom again.

Carol: Tell me more about that.

Shantel: All that wisdom I had at Washington, when I was acting and just being myself, I'd be able to get that back and use it to fight back here.

Carol: Can you give me an example of what you mean by using your wisdom to fight back?

Shantel: Sure, with my wisdom, I would be able to see through the things the girls are saying to me, and just go off and make my own friends.

Carol: What else?

Shantel: I'd be better at holding on to my comebacks when those evil lunch supervisors come around yelling at me, just look at them and smile or something and say, "Yes," and then get away from them and go sit somewhere else.

Carol: Wait, with your wisdom you'd be able to do that? "See through" the other girls' comments and not get all mad back at the lunch supervisors?

Shantel: Yeah, that's what I did at Washington. There were mean girls there, too. I just liked being there more, I guess.

Carol: So, let's take the miracle one step further, and let me ask your parents the same question. What would be the first sign that the miracle had happened and things were better for Shantel at school?

Mrs. D: Shantel would be happy to go to school and wouldn't be so hard to live with at home. [everybody laughs] I've got to be honest ...

Mr. D: You got that right, Shantel, if you got some wisdom somewhere that you lost, you really need to go get it. I'll drive you to go pick it up! [laughter again]

Solution-Focused Needs Assessment

One of the gaps in the present SFBT literature involves the application of SFBT to organizational and community contexts. One of the most prominent examples of a solution-focused community organization is Gonzalo Garza Independence High School, which we discussed in detail in Chapter 4. The notion of a solution-focused community organizer may sound far-fetched, but in fact, this is just what one of our colleagues became when she engaged in a series of solution-focused groups designed to help parents describe their goals for their children and the ways that they hoped that their neighborhood school could begin to address those needs.

Sarah is a social worker employed by a local community mental health agency in an urban Midwestern city. The goal of her community outreach unit is to facilitate partnerships with local schools in inner-city communities to increase parent/school involvement and also to generate more use of the agency's family-based mental health and vocational services. Despite having conducted needs assessment and service outreach for two years as part of a grant-funded project, Sarah and her colleagues were finding that their parent clients, many of whom had multiple challenges related to living in poverty, remained hard to reach and were not fully using the services offered by the agency. In a similar vein, school officials reported frustration with parents who did not participate in their child's education and seemed to only come to school when they "felt like it." These complaints are common to educators and practitioners trying to engage and involve parents coming from impoverished backgrounds (Comer, 2005).

As part of her startup work in a new neighborhood elementary school, Tillman, Sarah decided to conduct her agency's needs assessment in a new way. She spent a few days visiting local neighborhood businesses, churches, and organizations and compiled a list of 15 community stakeholders who were parents of students at Tillman and interested in coming to a focus group to discuss the agency's outreach program. When Sarah convened the group, she used the SFBT miracle question to help facilitate the discussion: "If a miracle happened overnight and Tillman became a place that was more welcoming to parents, what would be different?" The answers did not take long to surface. These parents said they spent most of their nonworking time taking care of young children, looking for employment, dealing with their own health issues at a range of different health care providers, or waiting at social welfare agencies to get their families services. Focus group members said the first thing that would be different is that the school would have agencies offering them help at school; in this way, they could also be more present at school for the students.

Sarah and the agency team then brainstormed with the parent focus group about the range of services that would be ideal to have available at Tillman and what format would best help them engage those services. The group agreed that having monthly "service fairs" on a particular day would help them to prioritize that day, and they also wondered whether this would help the school design a day or evening program for parents involving parent-teacher conferences and other activities. Significantly, Sarah decided not to include school faculty and administration in this initial meeting; the thinking was that parents would not be open in their comments and that school officials would be immediately put on the defensive. Subsequent meetings, however, did involve members of the focus group and school administration.

Sarah contacted several agencies that provided welfare and health care services to the community and was surprised at how eagerly they embraced the idea. (They wanted to do innovative outreach for their services and thought this was a fresh idea.) Within a month, the miracle question had helped create a little miracle at Tillman: a day-long "service fair" where parents could get health screenings, contact local social welfare agencies, and meet with their children's teachers. The service fairs have been held each month for the past year and are helping the administration at Tillman think about other ways they might reach out to parents whom they had previously thought of as indifferent to their children's education (Anderson-Butcher & Ashton, 2004).

SFBT Groups in Schools

Solutions to Anxiety

National survey data and health experts identify childhood anxiety as a growing and under-researched problem (American Academy of Child and Adolescent Psychiatrists, 2007). The literature on effective treatments for childhood anxiety emphasizes a combination of cognitive-behavioral therapy and pharmacological intervention (Chorpita & Southam-Gerow, 2006), though most researchers in this area acknowledge the need to further study the long-term impacts of anti-anxiety medication for children (Pollock & Kuo, 2004). One of the most promising areas of our recent practice has been efforts to work with students identified as having learning disabilities but also a host of anxiety symptoms associated with their school performance.

Box 6.1 describes an eight-week, solution-focused group intervention designed to help students coping with generalized anxiety disorder and those grappling with test anxiety. The group session was conducted with

Box 6.1 Eight-Week SFBT Group for Student Anxiety

Session 1: Introductions. Obtain informed consent for participation. Discuss group expectations. Discuss the goals of the group (i.e., to help students identify ways to manage their anxiety at home and school and to cope with test anxiety).

Session 2: In-session assignment. "What academic/school goals do you have this semester?" and "What do you hope to achieve by participating in this group for the next 8 weeks?" Use of the miracle question.

Session 3: Use of the scaling question (i.e., "On a scale from 1 to 10, with 1 being your academic/school goals not achieved 10 meaning all your goals have been achieved, where would you rate yourself as a student today?") Homework assignment for next week: "Where would you like to be on the scale at the end of the semester?" Appraise the group on "What are the ways in which you will accomplish this increase?" (Goal and future orientation.)

Session 4: Review Session 3 homework assignment. Group discussion on "signs of success" in achieving academic/school goals. Homework assignment for next week: First, "If I asked Mr./Ms._____, your _____ teacher, how he/she had witnessed these signs of success in your academic/school goals, what do you think he or she would say?" (i.e., the relationship question). Second, write down your signs of success in which you came closer to reaching your end of the semester score on the scale of 1 to 10.

Session 5: Review Session 4 homework assignment. Use the SFBT technique of EARS (i.e., Elicit, Amplify, Reinforce, and Start over). Use of the exception-finding question to amplify and reinforce present and future change.

Session 6: Revisit the scaling question. Homework assignment: A letter from the "older, wiser self" (Dolan, 1995). "Imagine that you have grown to be a healthy, wise old man or woman and you are looking back on this period of your life. What would this older and wiser man or woman suggest to you, which helped you get to where you are now in your academic/school goal(s)?"

Session 7: Review Session 6 homework assignment. Discuss how the "new" self has emerged: Employ EARS.
Session 8: Review Session 7 homework assignment. Discuss setbacks as being normal. Pass out certificates of success.

Source: Adapted from Newsome (2004).

students at a suburban, K-6 elementary school with a group of five fifth- and sixth-grade girls who either had been diagnosed with generalized anxiety disorder by outside mental health providers or had described significant anxiety to us during weekly sessions as part of their individualized education plan minutes. The group session was conducted at lunchtime for eight consecutive weeks, and sessions took place as students ate lunch and socialized with each other.

A Solution-Focused Parent Group for GRGs

The number of school-aged children living with their grandparents has increased in the past 20 years, with the 2000 US Census data reporting more than 4.5 million children in grandparent-headed households (Davies, 2002). This population of new "parents," who thought they had already finished being responsible for young children, is often assuming this new challenge under trying family, professional, and health circumstances (Fuller-Thomson & Minkler, 2000). To address the growing number of GRGs in our school community, we began to offer eight-week, solution-focused parenting groups specifically designed for GRGs, and we summarize of the content of those group sessions here.

The group model discussed here is an eight-week GRG "Solution Group." The group meets on school grounds, preferably at a time when most grandparents could attend. Although it is not absolutely essential that GRGs always be grouped separate from other parents/caregivers, we suggest that novice SFBT practitioners try to implement a group program for this specific population first, both to learn the specific needs of GRGs and to apply and test SFBT ideas with them.

The groups had the following topics for each week. Also included here are sample questions that we asked them at each weekly session as well as some examples of SFBT group interactions drawn from our previous work in this area (Newsome & Kelly, 2004). The first three weeks are held consecutively; after that, GRG groups take place on a two-week/monthly basis to emphasize the belief that GRGs can both support each other and act creatively and effectively on their own, without the aid of "experts" (Selekman, 1993).

Week 1: Introductions and Orientation to SFBT GRG Ideas

- What is the most important part of the problem that brought you here?
- What part of that problem would you like to work on first?
- What are your thoughts about the problem you're having with your grandchild?
- What is the one thing you would like to learn from this group as it relates to this problem?

As with any new group venture in a school, the first session is crucial. In this first session, we give grandparents a chance to get to know us, the other members in the group, and the basic ideas behind the SFBT approach. It is important to normalize both their particular circumstances as GRGs and the model collaborative problem solving between group members. Because change is going to be the focus of the group, we're also eager to discuss how SFBT views the change process and to contrast that with other, more deficit-based approaches. This approach allows us to immediately validate the GRGs for their experience and wisdom and to truly say that we believe they are the experts on matters concerning their grandchildren and that we hope to draw on their expertise over the course of the program.

Week 2: Identifying Your Signature Strengths as a Grandparent and Applying Them to Your Mission as a GRG

- What are your signature strengths as a grandparent raising your grandchild? (Peterson & Seligman, 2004)
- How do you use your signature strengths as a grandparent raising a grandchild?

In our second session, we ask group members to complete a strengths questionnaire to help us frame future discussions of their strengths as grandparents. Peterson and Seligman (2004) offer a taxonomy of "signature strengths" and virtues to complement the categories of psychopathology described in the *Diagnostic and Statistical Manual of Mental Disorders, Fourth Edition* and an instrument called the Values in Action (VIA) questionnaire that can be taken by the GRGs online. In this second session, we begin to use the VIA, along with written exercises and discussion, to help the group members analyze where and how they are using their strengths as a GRG.

Recently, the benefits of using the VIA were quite helpful with a GRG who had become the primary caregiver of her grandchildren. As such, the grandparent stated to the second author (Michael Kelly) that she was hesitant to use her artistic and imaginative ability (e.g., drawing, painting, building things, or making games out of chores) with her grandchildren because her daughter had raised them much more rigorously and harshly before she passed away. Through use of the VIA and a discussion that helped the grandparent identify her signature strengths, the GRG recognized that she could still honor her daughter's memory while also applying her creativity with her grandchildren (Newsome & Kelly, 2004, p. 73).

Week 3: Starting Small—How Small Changes Can Become Big Solutions

- Since our group has started, what have you noticed that is already different about the main problem you came in with?
- What did you do to make those changes?
- What do you need to do to maintain those changes with your grandchild?

An example of a conversation that took place with a GRG during the SFBT group process illustrates the use of the aforementioned questions:

> **Group Leader (GL):** Welcome back, everyone. Tonight, we want to start by discussing a time in the last three weeks that the problem or problems affecting your grandchild were not so overwhelming, and what you did as a grandparent to help ease or lessen those problems. Do we have anybody who can share with us tonight?
>
> **Ms. Valdez (MV):** I will. I think my grandson is getting better at school.
>
> **GL:** Really? Tell us how you know that.

MV: Well, my grandson was having trouble on the playground, getting in fights and all that, and they called me in.

GL: Who is "they" here that you're talking about?

MV: The school staff, they wanted him to stay off the playground.

GL: And all that was because they didn't think your grandson could handle being on the playground? Have you seen times when Juan could handle being on playgrounds with other kids?

MV: Yes, I told them he'll find his way, we just have to pay attention. To prove it I went to school to watch him play on the playground. I saw that he was alone, and nobody was playing with him. I thought, "No wonder he's getting in trouble; he's trying to find any way possible to fit in." I told him to go see if he could play soccer with some of the kids on the playground—he loves to play—and he did!

GL: And you were able to show the school that some kids can find their own way. You recalled how much your grandson loved playing soccer, and you helped him get in a game. And all that fighting stuff on the playground went away.

MV: Yep. All it took was a little attention. That's what these kids need, our attention.

The above vignette highlights how small changes can become big solutions. More importantly, the dialogue illustrates how the group leader and Ms. Valdez uncovered an exception of how the problem (i.e., fighting on the playground) became less debilitating to her grandson (i.e., when he started playing soccer with other kids on the playground). Similarly, it helped to increase the hope and resilience of Ms. Valdez as a primary caregiver to her grandson as she faces the many challenges and opportunities presented to her throughout the academic school year (Newsome & Kelly, 2004, pp. 75–76).

The first three weeks are held consecutively; after that, GRG groups take place on a two-week/monthly basis to emphasize the belief that GRGs can both support each other and act creatively and effectively on their own, without the aid of "experts" (Selekman, 1993).

- If you can imagine our final meeting and being able to rate your problem as being low, what will have changed between then and now?
- What is the first thing you might do as a grandparent raising a grandchild to make this change happen?
- On a scale from 1 to 10, with 1 being not coping at all with your new role and 10 being coping very well with your new role, how well would you say you are coping?
- What would be different in your life if you went from a 6 to a 7 or from a 7 to an 8?

A portion of a conversation we had with a GRG during a group session several years ago illustrates the use of the scaling question as a way to find exceptions:

> **Group Leader (GL):** Tonight, I'd would like you to think of something you've been working on changing with your grandchild. It can be something you've been working on at home or at school. I want you to rate how well you think your grandchild has been doing on a scale from 1 to 10, with 1 being very poor and 10 being very excellent. Would anyone like to start us off?
>
> **Ms. Wilson (MW):** My granddaughter, she has been fighting with her older brother too much, especially when it's time for them to get down to their schoolwork.
>
> **GL:** How would you rate her level of fighting with her brother in the last few weeks on a scale of 1 to 10, with 1 being very excessive and 10 being not excessive at all?
>
> **MW:** You know, I was thinking before you asked me. Early on, I would have said it was very excessive, I would have given her a 1, but lately, I'd say she's been making an effort. I think I would rate her at a 5, maybe a 6.
>
> **GL:** And that 5 or 6 is better than it was before?
>
> **MW:** Oh, yes! She was down around a 1 for too, too long.
>
> **GL:** What do you think brought her up from a 1 to 5?

MW: I've been just telling her to go to another room, and leaving it at that. I gave up yelling and cussing back at her—it didn't work. Besides, doing this gives her nobody to talk to and soon after she shapes up and starts saying, "Grandma, I'll be good, I promise."

GL: That's great. So, you're doing something different helps her decide to behave differently. What do you think needs to happen for your granddaughter to get to a 7 or 8?

MW: That would be amazing to see her at a 7 or 8. I think if she figures out that I'm serious about not letting her mess with her brother, she'll calm down. I can see her getting to that 7 or 8 someday.

In this vignette, the group leader used the scaling question with Ms. Wilson as a way to recognize the proactive change that had occurred over the last few weeks. More than that, however, the scaling question helped to open up a discussion of the progress and growth made by Ms. Wilson and her grandchild. By using the scaling question, the group leader was also able to tap into Ms. Wilson's practical wisdom in addressing a very common issue between two siblings (Newsome & Kelly, 2004, pp. 77–78).

Week 5: The "Doing Something Different Day": Using SFBT Interventions in Daily Life with Your Grandchildren

- What are two things you could do differently this week as a grandparent raising a grandchild as it relates to your problem?
- What are a few impacts you might imagine happening as a result of "doing something differently"?

Week 6: Maintaining Change: Ways to Keep Change Going as a GRG

- What are two things you did differently this week as a grandparent raising a grandchild that helped?
- What difference did it make as a result of you "doing something differently?"

- Looking back at your experience in this group at Week 1, what is different about your "parenting role?"
- Who in your life views you as a person who has wisdom to share?

For this session, we invite other GRG "elders" in the school community to share their wisdom in a panel discussion.

Week 8: Change Party: A Celebration of the Changes Already Made with the Help of SFBT and of Those Changes to Come

- What is new and powerful about you as a grandparent raising a grandchild?
- How can you maintain this new part of you as a grandparent raising a grandchild?
- What have you learned about your grandchild's strengths and capacity to change?
- What is the most important lesson you learned in this group, and who taught you this lesson?

In keeping with the SFBT philosophy, we choose to deal with group endings and termination issues by focusing on the positive aspects of the group. As a result, we have a "change party." In using the change party technique, each GRG brings his or her grandchildren to the group and shares one thing that has changed in the past three to four months as well as one strength they most admire about each of their grandchildren. (Each of the GRGs will have done a signature-strength VIA with each of his or her grandchildren at this point, to have that instrument to draw on.)

While the majority of this final group meeting is spent socializing and having fun, we do encourage the GRGs to consider forming some kind of informal network, with us or with other group members, to help build on the positive solutions and relationships that the group helped to foster (Newsome & Kelly, 2004, p. 80).

The Future

This is just a sampling of what a solution-focused school professional can do with SFBT ideas. What are your ideas after reading this chapter? Can you think of a place or population in your school community that might benefit from some solution-focused interventions? Starting small is a good idea; find a classroom or group of students and get started. After all, as we learned in Chapter 2, solution-focused practice teaches us that small changes can lead to big ones. Start small, start now; have fun with solution-focused work in your school!

References

Altshuler, S. J., & Kopels, S. (2003). Advocating in schools for children with disabilities: What's new with IDEA? *Social Work, 48*(3), 320–329.

American Academy of Child and Adolescent Psychiatrists. (2007). Facts on anxiety. Retrieved August 3, 2007, from http://www.aacap.org/cs/root/developmentor/advances_in_child_and_adolescent_anxiety_disorder_research

Anderson-Butcher, D., & Ashton, D. (2004). Innovative models of collaboration to serve children, youth, families, and communities. *Children & Schools, 26*(1), 39–53.

Anderson-Butcher, D., Iachini, A., & Wade-Mdivanian, R. (2007). *School linkage protocol technical assistance guide: Expanded school improvement through the enhancement of the learning support continuum.* Columbus, OH: College of Social Work, Ohio State University.

Bowen, G., Rose, R. A., & Bowen, N. K. (2005). *The reliability and validity of the school success profile.* Philadelphia: Xlibris Press.

Chorpita, B. F., & Southam-Gerow, M. (2006). Fears and anxieties. In E. J. Mash & R. A. Barkley (Eds.), *Treatment of child disorders* (3rd ed., pp. 271–335). New York: Guilford.

Comer, J. P. (2005). The rewards of parent participation. *Educational Leadership, 62*(6), 38–42.

Constable, R. (2006). *21st century school social work*: Plenary address at the Family and Schools Partnership Program, July 2006.

Davies, C. (2002). The Grandparent Study 2002 Report Research Report. Retrieved July 24, 2007, from http://www.aarp.org/research/family/grandparenting/aresearch-import-481.html

Dolan, Y. M. (1995). *Living a wonderful life: A solution-focused approach to help clients move beyond a survivor identify.* Workshop sponsored by the Brief Therapy Training Center of Canada, Toronto.

Epstein, M. H., & Sharma, J. M. (2004). *BERS-2 examiner's manual.* Austin, TX: Pro-Ed.

Fuller-Thomson, E., & Minkler, M. (2000). African American grandparents raising grandchildren: A national profile of demographic and health characteristics. *Health and Social Work, 25*, 109–118.

Gleason, E. (2007). A strength-based approach to the social developmental study. *Children & Schools, 29*(1), 51–59.

Hammond, C., & Reimer, M. (2006). Essential elements of quality after-school programs. Retrieved July 15, 2007, from http://www.cisnet.org/working_together/after-school.asp

House, A. (2002). *DSM-IV diagnosis in the schools.* New York: Guilford.

Murphy, J. (1996). Solution-focused brief therapy in the school. In S. Miller, M. Hubble, & B. Duncan (Eds.), *Handbook of solution-focused brief therapy* (pp. 184–204). San Francisco: Jossey-Bass Publishers.

Newsome, S. (2004). Solution-focused brief therapy (SFBT) group work with at-risk junior high school students: Enhancing the bottom-line. *Research on Social Work Practice, 14*(5), 336–343.

Newsome, W. S., & Kelly, M. (2004). Grandparents raising grandchildren: A solution-focused brief therapy approach in school settings. *Social Work with Groups, 27*(4), 65–84.

Peterson, C., & Seligman, M. E. P. (2004). *Character strengths and virtues: A classification and handbook.* New York: Oxford University Press.

Pollock, R., & Kuo, I. (2004). Treatment of anxiety disorders: an update. *Medscape International Congress of Biological Psychiatry Highlights of the International Congress of Biological Psychiatry,* 22–40.

Selekman, M. D. (1993). *Brief therapy solutions with difficult adolescents.* New York: Guildford Press.

Watkins, A. M., & Kurtz, P. D. (2001). Using solution-focused intervention to address African American male overrepresentation in special education: A case study. *Children & Schools, 23,* 223–235.

7

■ ■ ■

SFBT in Action

Child Abuse and Neglect

Robert Blundo & Kristin W. Bolton

Kids Are More than Victims: Abuse and Trauma in Schools

School social workers are faced with the important responsibility of helping students through many of life's current challenges, such as community violence, divorce, poverty, maltreatment, drug abuse, sexual abuse, sexting, and bullying. This chapter demonstrates ways of approaching and working with children who are faced with child maltreatment.

First, it is important to emphasis that the school social worker is *not the primary treatment person* in cases of neglect, abuse, or trauma. Yet, given that the school environment is one of the most significant settings for students outside of their home, school social workers do have an important part in reporting abuse and neglect, as well as in supporting students' ability not just to move on with their lives but also to thrive. An overarching responsibility of the school social worker is to help school staff better understand and appreciate the need for safety and trust within the school for all students and to assist the school in embracing a less authoritarian and zero tolerance atmosphere. Helping the students to feel *safe and trusted* by teachers, staff, and the school social worker will make it more likely that students will feel comfortable enough to reveal possible neglect and abuse and will aid in supporting the child once neglect or abuse has been verified (Bannink, 2014; Olson, 2014). Rather than focus on the abuse or neglect itself, providing a feeling of safety, along with helping the student to build trusting and supportive relationships within the school, is a significant event for any child confronting the trauma of neglect or abuse. Not only is this a potential restorative factor, it also creates a better chance that students will reveal something about their situation to a teacher, social worker or staff member.

This chapter also covers the following matters to better understand the position of a school social worker and students: 1) the context and pressures within school settings on student and staff, 2) how neuroscience research provides evidence for the need to create a school environment that provides a real sense of safety and caring within both the school and the social workers relationships with students, 3) a new appreciation of the student's life context and consequential developmental behaviors while in school, 4) the age distribution of students being engaged by school social workers, 5) the range of neglect and abuse issues to be considered, and 6) the challenges of being a designated reporter as well as a support for these children while in school.

Child Maltreatment in the United States

There are four major types of child maltreatment: 1) physical abuse, 2) sexual abuse, 3) emotional abuse, and 4) neglect. The National Child Abuse and Neglect Data System collects and analyzes data submitted by all 50 states, the Commonwealth of Puerto Rico, and the District of Columbia, and the data are reported to Congress by the US Department of Health and Human Services, Administration for Children and Families, Administration on Children, Youth, and Families Children's Bureau. The most recent data (from 2013) found that in the Unites States, there were 670,000 cases of child maltreatment (9.2 children per 1,000), and approximately 3.9 million children were the subjects of at least one report. Additionally, data revealed that in 2013, 9.0% of children classified as victims of maltreatment were found to be sexually abused, 79.5% were neglected, 18% were physically abused, and 8.7% were emotionally abused (Children's Defense Fund, 2014; US Department of Health and Human Services, 2013).

Bryant and Milsom (2005) found that school social workers are reporting the majority of cases, with elementary school social workers reporting significantly greater numbers of cases than high school social workers. The average age for first abuse 9.6 years for girls and 9.9 years for boys (US Department of Education, 2004). In response to the need for better protection, the Child Abuse and Treatment Act was passed by Congress in 1974. This law initiated the requirements for mandated reporting and definitions of abuse. Finally, the rates of abuse vary greatly state by state. For example, in 2013, child maltreatment rates ranged from 1.2 per 1,000 to 19.6 per 1,000 (CDF, 2014; US Department of Health and Human Services, 2013).

Neuroscience and Solution-Focused Engagement with Students

The consequences of neglect and abuse produce profound changes in the structure and functioning of the brain, with consequences for behavior and, in particular, relationships. A neurological perspective shifts the view of these behaviors to something more likely to be a defense against perceived threats. The hope here is that teachers, child protective workers, and school social workers are also shifting in how they view such behaviors. Rather than thinking "What is wrong with that child?" the neuroscience findings point to "What has happened to that child?" Beyond "what happened" is how the child will make it today and the following days, or how she or he might thrive in school and other settings. This is the area of supportive work where school social workers have an important role.

The descriptive term *neuroception* was coined by Stephen Porges (2011) to describe the non-conscious and instantaneous responses that occur every moment with regards to safety. All human beings are wired to detect safety or danger. The autonomic nervous system is on constant alert for safe and unsafe situations every quarter of a second. This enables the person to respond to unsafe situations faster than the thinking apparatus can make a decision whether to respond. This applies to all interactions with others, whoever they might be. Olson (2014) describes the neuroception of safety to occur when an individual senses other people as being accepting, non-judgmental, and helpful. When our neuroception registers a sense of being criticized, being rejected, or even just a sense of tension, anger, or fear from those round us, the experience of feeling vulnerable and unsafe is generated (Olson, 2014). We quickly experience a heightened sense of not being safe and not having trust in those around us. This is an idiosyncratic response of an individual who has been living with abuse or neglect. It is an automatic response and calls for defensive behaviors, such as yelling, hitting, fighting, shutting down, or running away. Thus, when students are living in an abusive, neglectful, or highly stressful environment, the experience is one of the world being unsafe and untrustworthy, even in the school.

When students lash out in anger or become withdrawn and unable to speak or talk, they are expressing a response to feeling unsafe. Abuse and neglect are obviously experiences that prime a student to one or all of these reactions. These actions on the part of the student are reflexive protective reactions that are initiated in a moment as fight, flight, or shutting down and withdrawing. More often than not, these responses are seen as disruptive classroom behavior: fighting or passivity, not responding, or seemingly being unable or just unwilling to speak. These are also behaviors and attitudes that draw the attention of school social workers. They may very well be signs of neglect or abuse as well as a consequence of living within a critically stressful community. The possible symptoms or signs of abuse and neglect are the same as those for students growing up in a dangerous community setting. Thus, the very behaviors that are seen as disruptive can be hints of neglect and abuse and/or adjustments to a traumatic environment. As noted, the conditions within the community are very likely confounding factors of physical and sexual abuse.

Finally, school social workers can benefit from continuing to understand the latest knowledge regarding neuroscience and trauma. Knowledge regarding the impact of trauma on the human brain is growing exponentially and provides insight for those who work closely with children exposed to trauma.

Importance of Safety and Trusting in Recovery and Thriving

SFBT is a key element in establishing a safe working relationship while dealing with issues of neglect or abuse and with students living in stressful communities. For now, the focus will be on a solution-focused approach to reporting suspected neglect or abuse and working to support students who have been found to be neglected or abused.

The issues of trust and safety are of prime importance in working with any student, particularly students experiencing child maltreatment. The solution-focused school social worker is especially suited for the formation of a safe setting by working with the student and his or her teachers. Solution-focused practice has an inherent capacity to create a safe working relationship. By attending to client strengths rather than problems, seeing children as having possibilities of recovery and thriving, and considering students as experts on their own life experiences and then creating a focus on movement toward successes, survivorship, and thriving, the school social worker helps students create their own picture of the desired outcome and better future, even if in very small ways. Contrary to many forms of trauma treatment, solution-focused practice, while acknowledging the pain and fear of neglect and abuse, shifts its attention to those moments, exceptions, or instances when the student is able, in small ways, to demonstrate the ability to thrive in the midst of the chaos. Significantly, solution-focused practice appreciates the perceptions of students and acknowledges the anger and pain expressed in their behaviors in school. It believes in the student's ability to conceive of a better life as the expert on that life. At the same time, solution-focused practice trusts in the student's ability to focus on those moments when things have been or are going a little better, a little safer, and the student is more likely to feel trust.

SFBT provides a student with a safe conversation by being carefully listened to, having ideas and beliefs affirmed as being the student's sense of the situation, and having hints of possibilities noticed by the social worker and reinforced, both by the acknowledgment and by looking closer at the student's perceptions as a means of working within the student's own frame of awareness. The following are keys to affirmative relationships with students (Berg & Steiner, 2003, p. 131):

1. Rather than a lecture, challenge, or attempt to persuade ... develop a trusting relationship or one in which the school social worker truly believes the child to have he capacity to thrive and trusts in the child.
2. Trusting the student's ideas of what they think would be best or helpful now while at school.
3. Focus on the present and immediate future.
4. Keep focus on actions and not on gaining insights.
5. Pay attention to what is working, even a little bit, to help create possible solutions or better outcomes. (p. 131)

Although therapy to treat abused children is not the school social worker's function, the following solution-focused factors can be very helpful in building a sense of trust and safety, leading to increased possibilities for thriving:

1. Even abused children, no matter how badly they have been abused, still have areas that are functioning well.
2. You should begin with the healthy part of the child.
3. You should ask children about what is their idea of how they want their life/situation to be different so that life is a little bit better for them; sometimes they, too, like all children, have an idea of what they want their life to be like.

Although Berg and Steiner (2003) are referring to actual treatment work with abused children, the same supportive and relationship building skills are a key to supportive work done by school social workers.

Being a Mandated Reporter

The complexities of identifying possible abuse make the position of teachers and school social workers very difficult. The social worker may need to act as the mandated reporter and/or as support for students maintaining themselves within the school setting after having been engaged in child protective services and possible foster care. These factors change the nature of the work being done by the school social worker and the relationship the social worker may (or may not) have with the student. The responsibility of either making or not making a report can be problematic for teachers and social workers. If reports turn out to be erroneous, the reporters can face court action for making false allegations; if reports are not made, the reporters can face court action not making a report as well (Brown, Brack, & Mullis, 2008).

Therefore, this position presents a daunting task to any school social worker. Two related elements are the ongoing relationship a school social worker had with the child before any incidence of abuse or neglect and maintaining that relationship following a substantiated or unsubstantiated report. Both conditions of having made a report will have an impact on the student's relationship with the school social worker and the parents.

Reporting a possible neglect or abuse incident challenges the relationship between the student and social worker. Maintaining a working and trusting relationship is important, as we have seen, to the social worker remaining a supportive and trusted adult in the school setting. When in a position of being a mandated reporter, it is important to have a set of simple standards that would justify reporting. These standards would vary depending on the age of the student and the nature of the available information. Berg and Steiner (2003) state that it is important not to be overly protective in an effort to avoid making things worse. At the same time, it is important that any contact with the student not be confrontational or argumentative. They add that if the situation is immediate and extremely cruel or violent, in which by the student needs immediate attention and protection, the mandated reporter must engage the authorities right away and provide for the care of the child until protection is made possible.

In many cases, the school social worker is faced with limited information and possibly conflicting stories. Obviously, the school social worker needs to follow whatever guidelines have been established with their local child protective services. The decision to report a suspicious set of information should be made in consultation with the teacher and other staff. Berg and Kelly (2000) provide several basic assessment points that the school social worker would need to be prepared to answer:

> Is the reported neglect or abuse one of a crisis, such as the child comes to school with physical marks of abuse, a child reports that he or she was physically abused, or (there is some corroboration of the abuse) by a witness.
> Has the (social worker) witnessed the actual events or signs of abuse or neglect? (p. 58)

Otherwise, it is important for the school social worker to view students' in the following ways:

1. Every abused child, no mater how badly they have been abused, still have areas that are functioning well. (Berg & Steiner, 2003, p. 131)
2. You should begin with the healthy part of the child first. (Berg & Steiner, 2003, p. 131)
3. You should engage students in terms of what will make their experience better during school. Remember that as a school social worker, you are not there to provide treatment but, rather, to offer what might better be called SFBT coaching. Coaching is focused upon supporting the student in creating a more positive, safer atmosphere and success in school. Building on his or her strengths and abilities along with support during difficult moments would be most helpful effort during these times.
4. Rogers (1951) stressed that with genuine trust, empathy, and authenticity expressed in the contact with the social worker, the client gains a sense of feeling felt, a sense of being heard and appreciated. It is very important the social worker is not disingenuous but, rather, has learned to truly trust and believe in the client's ability to make it and succeed. Given the tumultuous nature of schools and classrooms, where performance evaluations loom over teachers and school social workers, it is not easy to maintain this position. (Carkuff & Berenson, 1967)

Mandated Reporting and Beyond

Whether the situation involves neglect, physical abuse, or sexual abuse changes the work that is done with the students and others who may be involved, such as child protective services, courts, families, and treatment facilities. These students will be unduly impacted by the pressure to perform academically and behaviorally and may already be experiencing difficulties, which may have brought them to the attention of the school social worker in the first place. If the school social worker has been having contact with these students, the possibility of initiating an abuse report challenges the relationship between the social worker and student.

Ratner and Yusuf (2015) state that at times when there is probable harm, the school social worker may be required to step out of the SFBT approach. To determine if the situation of the child meet the basic requirement for mandated reporting will require specific non-SFBT questions about the circumstances. They demonstrate this by providing an example of a child's response to the best hopes question. In this case, the child answered that "It would stop," and to further future-oriented outcome questions, the same response was given. Stepping away from SFBT, the child was asked what "It" meant. When the child revealed bullying, assessment questions followed to determine what specifically was happening to help protect the child from further harm: As Ratner and Yusuf (2015) explain:

> When safety is an issue, whether from bullying, self-harm, substance misuse and so on, [the school social worker] has to make a decision as to whether he or she needs to refer on to someone who can deal more effectively with the situation. . . . Serious decisions should where ever possible be taken in conjunction with another colleague [also, in case of abuse, to the mandated services]. (p. 19)

As a mandated reporter, the solution-focused school social worker has an obligation to report suspected abuse or neglect. The reporting process varies and is based on the gathering of facts and possible evidence that creates suspicion. If abuse, in particular sexual abuse, has been verified, a specially trained therapist will take on the actual trauma work necessary for the child's recovery. Importantly, however, the solution-focused school social worker can assist in the child's survivorship through ongoing conversations focused on competencies as well as maintaining normal expectations and support of day-to-day accomplishments. SFBT offers an opportunity to engage students and teachers in a positive and appreciative manner during the briefest contact. The interaction turns from focusing on problems and weaknesses to strengths and possibilities built around positive, supportive relationships. SFBT is particularly unique in that its use encourages the affirmative relationships necessary for meaningful change as well as a sense of safety and trust, allowing for the revealing of suggestive material to the school social worker. Relationships are the very essence of human development and required throughout life for there to be meaningful growth in any working relationship (Frank & Frank, 1991; Hubble, Duncan & Miller, 1999).

Given this, the question becomes how to maintain a supportive and compassionate relationship while obtaining information to help substantiate making a report and/or while being supportive of survivorship. Every student is different, and students at every age are different in how they are able to communicate or respond to inquiries about what they have been experiencing that involves important people, such as family members or other "trusted individuals." One important way to do what, specifically, is to maintain the SFBT position of accepting the student's perceptions and trusting the student to share what is comfortable at the time while recognizing the likely feelings of guilt and shame in revealing the trauma narrative. The school social worker need not become the interrogator in an attempt to verify the report. That is the work of the child protective services worker and the child's future therapist. Much will depend on prior relationships between the school social worker and the student, if one existed before this conversation. Let the student realize that you are not embarrassed, ashamed, upset, or disbelieving of what they are telling you through body language, facial expressions, and comments. Your focus is on supporting the student by acknowledging how hard it must be to reveal this situation. It is important that the student feel listened to and trusted.

In the following interview, a student, Beth, is assisted in revealing an incident of sexual abuse:

> **School Social Worker (SSW):** I'm glad we could meet; you
> sounded very concerned about something important to you.
> How can our meeting be helpful to you?
> **Beth:** Umm ... yea ... [looking around the office] you know
> I have never been a really good student. I haven't been

---

coming to school that much lately, and I'm not doing good in my classes, like we talked about last week.

SSW: Yes, you've been able to get to school sometimes but not as much as you may want. I'm impressed, though, with how you are at least trying to make it to school these last few weeks since we talked. There must be a lot going on that makes it harder for you to come to school as much as you would like. I'm curious; is there anything that would be helpful to talk about that might help even a little bit?

Beth: Maybe . . . I don't know if I can . . . not sure . . .it is very hard and I don't know what will happen if I talk about it.

SSW: Well, in what way do you think it might help if you did share it with me or someone else? Do you think it would make things better for you . . . like feeling like coming to school?

Beth: I don't know. It might make things even worse.

SSW: It must be very important to you if it might make things worse. Even though it sounds like if you were to get some help with this issue, it might make your life easier in doing the things you seem to want to do, like school. That is a tough place to be. What would be the most helpful for us to do that might help move you to a better place and feeling better?

At this point, notice how the student jumps in and starts to share her experience, as if possibly the social worker's acceptance and support gave her the trust to jump into the situation.

Beth: It's my older uncle . . . He comes over a lot and stays with us, and sometimes my mom leaves us with him when she goes out. I liked him, but last semester he stayed over and he wanted to kiss me. I didn't know what to do. My mom likes him a lot, and they are close. Now, he says he loves me, and he has put his hands on me, you know, my breasts. I just stood there and didn't know what to do. I don't want to let mom know; she would be mad at me.

SSW: Thank you for taking the chance and trying to help your situation by sharing it with me. I understand how difficult it must have been for you keeping this secret and trying to protect your mom's relationship with her brother. I admire your courage to take care of yourself given the very difficult situation you've been in. Do you have any ideas about how you would want to make this better and not have this happening?

Beth: I'm aware of child protective services. They see some of my friends and their families. I don't want to have to leave my mom, and I don't want her to be mad at me.

SSW: I agree that you should be able to stay in your home and also to have a good relationship with your mom. You are aware of child protective services. It is their job to help protect you and any other young person. I agree with you that it is best when you stay at home and make it a safe place for you and your brothers and sisters and your mom, too. From what you have shared, it would be important to contact child protective services. I know several people there, and I would like for you to help me make this contact so that you can make your home safe. Will you help make that happen?

Beth: I guess ... But I'm still afraid of what mom might say and of her brother.

SSW: I understand your not wanting to upset your mom or even your uncle. It's not an easy decision to make. What do you think would be the best way to handle this so that you don't have to deal with your uncle's behavior and you can feel safe?

Beth: Do you think the service worker would help me tell my mother and help make things easier after she finds out?

SSW: I can only say that that is exactly the work they do with families in these situations. It's important that you are safe and that your family can continue to be close. And it's important that the worker understand what happened and then has your help in finding the best way to work with your mom. You can meet and talk with the worker here at school and help her understand the situation. Is that okay with you?

Beth: Yes, if I can see her first ... Okay.

SSW: Let me call her right now and let you know how this is going to work. The basic idea is to be able to let your mother know what has happened and help her deal with her brother and be supportive of you. I will be available here at school so that I can help support what you have decided to do to make things better.

First and foremost, being a mandated reporter, the social worker would need to make the report even if the child did not want that to happen. Yet, it is always important to help the student have a say in what may happen and be aware of the help being initiated. If or when substantiation occurs, the social worker's challenge is maintaining an appreciative and helpful relationship with the student. Contact would generally acknowledge the difficulties but focus on what the child can confirm as being helpful in making their life more manageable during school. By having the student state what it will take to keep going at this point, the social worker has validated the student's competencies at whatever level Beth is able to manage. Whether those competencies are attending classes, doing homework, talking with friends, not fighting as much, or being less sad, all can be appreciated for what they mean for recovery. Using scaling question may or may not feel appropriate; if used, they can provide additional supportive evidence of success.

The next case example illustrates how to use relationship and scaling questions for a high school student who was removed from her biological parents due to abuse and neglect and has recently been placed in her second foster care home. Since the student has a social service caseworker and a therapist, the responsibility of the school social worker is to focus on success in school rather than on the abuse and neglect the student experienced at home. The school social worker also should assist the student in forming supportive relationships with others. This high school student has been trying to study for a test but is struggling with confidence issues and worried about passing the test. The following example shows how to help with her gain confidence and, more importantly, how scaling questions can help reinforce the supportive relationships that exist in the student's school environment:

Jackie: I'm not sure if I can pass the test. I have trouble thinking clearly. Ms. Jason, my teacher, says I can. I just don't know.

SSW: So, Ms. Jason says she thinks you can do it. What do you think she knows about you that tells her that you can do this?

Jackie: I don't know. I couldn't say.

SSW: You have known Ms. Jason for, what, about three semesters now? If we were to ask Ms. Jason, what do you think she would say?

Jackie: Yea, I've had her for most of my English classes. She's usually nice, and I've done okay in her classes.

SSW: I'm wondering where you think Ms. Jason would place you on a scale. What I mean is if she were to use a scale from 1 to 10, with 1 meaning that there is no way at all for you to just pass and 10 meaning she believes you can do very well on the exam, where do you think she would place you on that scale?

Jackie: Umm, not sure, maybe at a 7. She really believes I can do a lot better than I do.

SSW: So, a 7. That's pretty good. Ms. Jason must think very highly of you and your abilities. What do you think gives her that idea?

Jackie: I guess I've done pretty well in her classes, even when things at home were not very good. I like English, and I like Ms. Jason. I've tried harder in her class. Most of the time I've been able to get a good grade.

SSW: How would you make that happen? I mean, try harder and make a good grade, not the highest grade but one you would say was a good effort.

Jackie: It would help if I talked over my material with Ms. Jason. That's helped before, and I think she would do it. I just need to ask her.

SSW: So, how would you make that happen?

Jackie: I can just talk with her before or after class. She's usually available then.

SSW: That sounds like a good plan. Let's see what you can do, and maybe we can talk later this week, if that is okay with you.

Jackie: I'll give it a shot today. I have her class in fourth period.

SSW: Sounds good, see you later this week.

The above example probably sounds like an avoidance of the issues of neglect or abuse. But remember, the school social worker is not engaging in treatment; rather, the effort is to build on the student's strengths and abilities to thrive and do as best she can. Using scaling and having the student focus on what she thinks the teacher would rate her is intentional. Not only does the school social worker help the student to provide a sense of her own place on the scale, the student is also being helped to strengthen her relationship with an important person who cares about her and believes in her ability. In the example above, it is a favorite teacher who provides her with safety and with possibilities of success. This is a necessary experience for a child who has been neglected in many ways and most likely feels abandoned by others. Losing a sense of trust and safety must be addressed by helping to build trust and support and safety in the school—or even by just one teacher and/ or the school social worker. The very fact of being focused on a potentially positive effort and, importantly, helping the student to build a stronger and supportive relationship with an adult is a significant factor in building the sense of trust and safety that is reparative of the unsafe experiences in her home placement experiences.

What about the lingering consequences of verified abuse at home and several foster care homes, however? Ironically, if this student has remained within the same school district, then that school likely is the only consistent and familiar place she has. What is important for this young woman is the ability to move on in her life and to feel supported and cared about by other adults. By acknowledging the difficult circumstances in a manner suitable for the student's age and focusing on how the child is making it, at least in school and obviously not without pain, the idea of survivorship is being laid down, and school can be seen as a respite from the possible turmoil at home or foster care.

The school social worker clearly has restrictions on what he or she can do. When a report has been made and substantiated, the school social worker must focus on the child in the context of the school setting. Protective services will be involved with the family, and a professional therapist or agency specializing in abuse counseling will be working with the child on recovery. However, the child may prefer the only person who has been there for them in other ways: the solution-focused school social worker. Students who come to the attention of the school staff concerning neglect or abuse more often than not have had some form of contact with the school social worker. This may provide an initial sense of safety for sharing material that becomes the cause of a report, and following a report, the school social worker may be is recognized as a safe person to talk with about having some success at school, even if just a little bit.

The age of the student will change the nature of practice, with different forms of interaction and levels of understanding on the part of the student and the school social worker. With an elementary-age cohort, the school social worker will be faced with a wide range of maturity and communication skills. These students differ from middle school students, and even more so from high school students. The growing transitions in physical, emotional, and social development reflect the elementary, middle, and high school grades.

Berg and Steiner (2003) as well as Berg and Kelly (2000) demonstrate in their work that even the youngest child has some idea about what will make his or her life better and safe. These authors list such ideas as children wishing for a parent or a grandparent to be with them more often at home, not to have to stay with an aunt, to have friends, not be bullied, not have to come to school . . . and the list goes on. It is very important to try to find out their desired outcome by asking them clarifying questions. The following session with James, a 10-year-old boy and the oldest child in a family with four children, provides an example:

> **SSW:** Hi, James, good to see you here today. Thanks for coming down from class to see me.
> **James:** Am I in trouble or something?
> **SSW:** Not at all. You are not in any trouble. Your teacher, Ms. Jason, told me that you had hurt yourself somehow. She saw the bruises on your arms and wanted the nurse and me to make sure you are okay. Ms. Johnson [the school nurse], will see if she can help make them feel better. I haven't seen you for a few weeks. I see that you have a Star Wars shirt on; who is your favorite person in the movie?

James: I like Chewbacca.

SSW: Yeah, I like him, too. What do like about him?

James: He's real strong and a friend of the other guy in the spaceship.

SW: He is a good friend and helps his friend. Who would you say is your best friend?

James: I guess it was Will. We moved away last summer, and I haven't been able to see him.

SSW: I'm sorry that you had to move away from your friend. I bet he is missing you, too. What happened that you had to move away from Will?

James: My father left and my mom and us had to move to another house.

SSW: That's a lot of changes. How have you been able to make new friends?

James: I haven't really made friends like Will. I play with some of the guys my age. Mom wants me to stay more with my brothers and sister because she is working a lot now since my Dad left.

SSW: It sounds like you have more responsibilities now, too, watching over your brothers and sister. Taking care of them must not be easy. How do you do that?

James: Well, sometimes it doesn't work out, and I get into fights with my brothers. That's how this happened [pointing to his arm]. They don't want to listen. They get mad, and we fight a lot.

SSW: So you got the bruises from fighting with your brothers.

James: Sometimes with my sister, too.

SSW: Wow, do they get hurt, too?

James: Sometimes, but it is mostly me. The are hitting me, and they hit my arms.

SSW: Wow, I can see how hard that must be for you. So, what do you think would make things better? You know, so that you would not have to fight with your brothers and sister.

James: I guess if mom didn't have to work so much, and she would be home.

SSW: So, how would mom being home earlier help you keep from fighting with your brothers and sister?

Solution-Focused Brief Therapy in Schools

James: I wouldn't have to keep them from going outside, keeping them in the house.

SSW: That must be very hard to do. I can see how it might turn into a fight. So, what would be different if mom was home earlier?

James: Most of the time they listen to her, and she can get them stop playing and eat.

SSW: I can see that you have a lot to do when your mom is working late. How did you learn to try and help out like that?

James: I don't know. I just do it, I guess.

SSW: Well, it's not easy to try and keep your brothers and sister in the house. Most kids like to run around outside after school. Are you trying to help your mom by trying to keep the kids inside?

James: Yeah, she works a lot.

SSW: I can see that you care about your mom a lot and are trying to help. Kind of like Chewbacca. That is a very important responsibility for a young man to take on. I'm wondering, James, can you think of anything that would help you and your mom to take care of the home when she is working?

James: I don't know.

SSW: Well, has there been any time when your mom is working that you didn't have to fight with your brothers and sister to stay inside?

James: Maybe when my cousin comes over. She's older, and they listen better to her.

SSW: So, when your older cousin comes over, it sounds like she is a lot of help for you and your mom.

James: Yeah, I can do what I want to and not fight my brothers and sister.

SSW: That sounds like a much better situation for you and your brothers and sister. I would like to ask you if it would be alright to contact a person I know that works with families to help out in making things little better. If I call her, she would like to speak with you and your mom to see how things might be a little better for you and your mom.

James: I guess so.

SSW: I can see that your mom loves all of you and is working very hard to take care of you all. I'm sure that the person I call can meet with you and your mom to see what can be done to make it so you don't need to get into fight with your brothers and sister. Is that okay with you?

James: I guess.

SSW: I will get a note to you after I call and let you know what is happening. I'm sure that Chewbacca would want that, too. I'll see you later today to let you know what will happen. I'll walk you back to class now.

The interview just described could be more direct—that is, by asking James how he got the bruises first and gone from there. For instance: "James, what happened? How did you get all those bruises?" Then, the work would become focused on understanding the problem by gathering details of and facts about what was taking place in the home. This seems to be the typical way to have the conversation. Yet, Bannink (2014) notes that it is a "misconception that there can only be sufficient acknowledgment if the problem is wholly dissected and analyzed or if the client is afforded every opportunity to expatiate [or expound] on his or her view of the problem" (p. 75). Importantly, it might not have been such a full story as we just had with James. The solution-focused approach attempts to build a relationship that makes it more likely the student will reveal more information. This can lead to a better understanding and to potential resources, such as James' cousin. It appears that James is a responsible child, even though he gets into fights with his siblings. He does provide a reasonable description of what might be considered neglect and has given a possible focus on what child protective services might want to look into. Connecting with child protective services might also help James' mother in terms of child care and other family services.

Conclusion

The fundamental posture of the school social worker is one of acceptance and support of all students. This is especially important for children who grow up within a neglectful or abusive home environment since they are very likely to demonstrate a range of behaviors. SFBT can be a useful approach when engaging students who are victims of child maltreatment. The solution-focused techniques have the potential to create positive experiences for children who have mostly experienced maltreatment at home. Finally, it is critical that the school social worker focus on creating a safe support system for the students, which can play an important role in helping students to move forward in their lives.

References

Bannink, F. (2014). *Post traumatic success: Positive psychology & solution-focused strategies to help clients survive & thrive*. New York, NY: Norton.

Berg, I. K., & Kelly, S. (2000). *Building solutions in child protective services*. New York, NY: Norton.

Berg, I. K., & Steiner, T. (2003). *Children solution work*. New York, NY: Norton.

Brown, S. D., Brack, G., & Mullis, F. Y. (2008). Traumatic symptoms in sexually abused children: Implications for school social workers. *Professional School Counseling, 11*(6), 368–379. http://dx.doi.org/10.5330/PSC.n.2010-11.368

Bryant, J., & Milsom, A. (2005). Child abuse reporting by school social workers. *Professional School Counseling, 9*(1), 63–71.

Carkuff, R., & Berenson, B. (1967). *Beyond counselling and therapy*. New York, NY: Holt.

Children's Defense Fund. (2014). *The state of America's children 2014 report*. Washington, DC: Children's Defense Fund. Retrieved from www.childrensdefense.org/library/state-of-americas-children.

Frank, J. D., & Frank, J. (1991). *Persuasion and healing: A comparative study of psychotherapy*. Baltimore, MA: Johns Hopkins University Press.

Hubble, M. A., Duncan, B. L., & Miller, S. D. (1999). *The heat & soul of change: What works in therapy*. Washington, DC: American Psychological Association.

Olson, K. (2014). *The invisible classroom*. New York: Norton.

Porges, S. W. (2011). The Polyvagal Theory: Neurophysiological foundations of emotions, attachment, communication, and self-regulation. New York, NY: Norton.

Ratner, H., & Yusuf, D. (2015). *Brief coaching with children and young people: A solution focused approach*. New York, NY: Routledge.

Rogers, C. R. (1951). *Client-centered therapy: Its current practice, implications and theory*. Boston, MA: Houghton Mifflin.

US Department of Education, Office of the Undersecretary. (2004). *Educator sexual misconduct: A synthesis of existing literature*. Washington, DC: US Department of Education.

US Department of Health and Human Services, Administration for Children and Families, Administration on Children, Youth and Families, Children's Bureau. (2013). *Child maltreatment 2012*. Washington, DC: US Department of Health and Human Services. Retrieved from http://www.acf.hhs.gov/sites/default/files/cb/cm2012.pdf

8

![decorative squares]

SFBT in Action
Mental Health and Suicidal Ideation

Carol Buchholz Holland

Prevalence of Youth Mental Health Issues

Child and adolescent mental health issues continue to be a major concern for schools throughout the United States. After reviewing youth mental health statistics, it is understandable why schools are diligently searching for effective ways to meet student mental health needs. For example, in 1999, the US Department of Health and Human Services (USDHHS) published the *Mental health: A report of the Surgeon General*, which found that approximately "20% of children are estimated to have mental disorders with at least mild functional impairment" (p. 46). Friedman et al. (1996; as cited in USDHHS, 1999, p. 46) also estimated that approximately 5% to 9% percent of children ages 9 to 17 would meet the criteria for "serious emotional disturbance." A 2013 report by the Centers for Disease Control and Prevention (CDC) additionally found that "a total of 13% [to] 20% of children living in the United States experience a mental disorder in a given year" (p. 2).

A comprehensive study conducted by Merikangas et al. (2010) presented a breakdown of mental health disorders experienced by US adolescents (ages 13–19) and found that 31.9% of adolescents in their study met the criteria for an anxiety disorder, which included Agoraphobia, Generalized Anxiety Disorder, Social Phobia, Specific Phobia, Panic Disorder, Post-traumatic Stress Disorder, and Separation Anxiety Disorder. Merikangas et al. also found that 8.3% of the total adolescent study sample met the criteria for severe anxiety disorders. In addition, 14.3% of the adolescents in the study were affected by mood disorders, such as Major Depressive Disorder,

Dysthymia, and Bipolar I or II, and 11.2% of the total sample were considered to have severe cases of mood disorders. Prevalence of behavior disorders, such as Attention-Deficit Hyperactivity Disorder, Oppositional Defiant Disorder, and Conduct Disorder, was also assessed. The researchers noted that 19.6% of the adolescents in the study met the criteria for a behavior disorder and that 9.6% of these adolescents were considered to have severe behavior disorders.

Merikangas et al. (2010) also reported information regarding the average onset of specific mental disorders for adolescents in the study who met the criteria for a disorder. Their results indicated that 50% of the adolescents who met the criteria for anxiety disorders had their onset by age 6, 50% who met the criteria for mood disorders had their onset by age 13, and 50% who met the criteria for behavior disorders had their onset by age 11. In addition, the incidence rate for major depression and dysthymia nearly doubled from 13 to 14 years of age to from 17 to 18 years (Merikangas et al., 2010). Furthermore, the National Alliance on Mental Illness (NAMI) (2014) issued a report stating that "half of all long-term mental illness begins by age 14 and three quarters emerges by age 24" (p. 17). These statistics demonstrate the importance of providing comprehensive mental health prevention and intervention programs in schools because the age of onset for mental health disorders often occurs during the elementary or middle school years.

In the latest national Youth Risk Behavior Survey (YRBS) report of students in grades 9 through 12 who attend either public or private schools in the United States, 29.9% of the surveyed students indicated that they "had felt so sad or hopeless almost every day for 2 or more weeks in a row that they stopped doing some usual activities" sometime during the 12 months before completing the survey (USDHHS, 2014, p. 11). In addition, survey results indicated that "17.0% of students had seriously considered attempting suicide during the 12 months before the survey" and that 13.6% of the students "had made a plan about how they would attempt suicide" (USDHHS, 2014, pp. 11–12). Although survey results between 1991 and 2009 showed decreases for these statistics, results between 2009 and 2013 revealed increases in the percentage of students who indicated that they had seriously considered attempting suicide (13.8% to 17%) and that they had made a suicide plan (10.9% to 13.6%). The 2013 survey also reported that 8% of students "had attempted suicide one or more times during the 12 months before the survey," an increase from the 2009 survey that had revealed 6.3% of students indicated they had attempted suicide (CDC, n.d.-c,

p. 1). It is uncertain whether data collected from the 2015 YRBS will continue to show increases in student responses for these survey items. Recent statistics provided by the National Center for Health Statistics, however, show that suicide is now ranked as the second-leading cause of death for individuals ages 15 to 24 (the leading cause being unintentional injury) (CDC, n.d.-a). Before 2011, suicide had been ranked for several years as the third-leading cause of death for individuals ages 15 to 24 (CDC, n.d.-b).

The number of students who need additional services is a growing concern for schools. Because the stigma associated with mental health problems still exists in our society, some students and their families may be reluctant to seek these services outside of the school setting (Murphey, Barry, & Vaugh, 2013). This continued reluctance strengthens the case for providing school-based mental health services. Although most schools do not have unlimited resources, they are often the main provider of mental health services for children (Hoagwood & Erwin, 1997). In many cases, schools are the first place where student mental health issues are identified and addressed. Erford, Newsome, and Rock (2007) stressed that students with mental health needs who do not receive assistance may develop more serious issues, which could have significant negative impacts on their education. For example, untreated mental health problems could result in poor academic performance or even the decision to drop out of school. In addition, untreated mental health issues could result in even more serious safety concerns, such as harm to self or others. The December 2014 report by the NAMI noted that "children and youth who receive prompt, effective mental health care demonstrate surprising resilience, overcoming major challenges to thrive in school, home and the community" (pp. 17–18). As a result, it is important for schools to take the lead in providing effective prevention, early identification, and early intervention of student mental health concerns.

Student Risk and Protective Factors

After a serious review of youth mental health statistics, bills for the Mental Health in Schools Act of 2015 were introduced in the U.S. House of Representatives (H.R. 1211) and Senate (S. 1588) during 2015 (Congress. gov, 2015a, 2015b). These bills proposed an amendment to the current Public Health Service Act. Part of this amendment included the requirement of comprehensive school-based mental health programs that use a public health approach and are designed to assist children who have experienced trauma and violence. Fortunately, there has been movement away from using the traditional disease model in schools, which only provides treatment after an illness has occurred (O'Connell, Boat, & Warner, 2009). Instead, schools have shifted more toward utilizing prevention and intervention models, which are designed to strengthen resiliency by building capacity and to identify risk and protective factors.

Rak and Patterson (1996) defined resiliency as "the capacity of those who are exposed to indentifiable risk factors to overcome those risks and avoid negative outcomes such as delinquency and behavioral problems, psychological maladjustment, academic difficulties, and physical complications" (p. 368). In addition, Galassi and Akos (2007) noted that "resiliency research has repeatedly demonstrated that, contrary to popular belief, most people are not permanently overwhelmed by and irreparably damaged by exposure to life circumstances" (p. 33). Strengths-based approaches such as the solution-focused approach are bolstered by resiliency research findings supporting the belief that human beings have "self-righting tendencies that move children toward normal adult development under all but the most persistent adverse circumstances" (Werner & Smith, 1992, p. 202). These "self-righting tendencies" align with the solution-focused assumption that all people are capable of change. In other words, resiliency is a part of the "healthy human development" process (Bernard, 1991, p. 18).

While examining methods for developing the capacity of individuals, risk factors and protective factors are also considered. The Massachusetts Executive Office of Health and Human Services (MEOHHS) identified five domains in which risk and protective factors are categorized. These domains include individual, peer, family, school, and community/society (MEOHHS, n.d.). O'Connell et al. (2009) defined a risk factor as "a characteristic at the biological, psychological, family, community, or cultural level that precedes and is associated with a higher likelihood of problem outcomes" (p. xxviii). Examples of risk factors associated with adolescent suicidal behavior include aggressive and violent behavior (Walrath et al., 2001), alcohol and other illicit drug use (King et al., 2001; Wichstrom, 2000), anxiety (Groholt, Ekeberg, Wichstrom, & Haldorsen, 2000; Ruchkin, Schwab-Stone, Koposov, Vermeiren, & King, 2003), experiencing or witnessing violence (Brown, Cohen, Johnson, & Smailes, 1999; Ruchkin et al., 2003), family distress (Breton,Tousignant, Bergeron, & Berthiaume, 2002; King et al., 2001), hopelessness (Csorba et al., 2003; Perkins & Hartless, 2002), and risk behaviors (Beautrais, 2001; Fergusson, Beautrais, & Horwood, 2003; Gray et al., 2002; King et al., 2001).

O'Connell et al. (2009) also defined a protective factor as "a characteristic at the biological, psychological, family, or community (including peers and culture) level that is associated with a lower likelihood of problem outcomes or that reduces that negative impact of a risk factor on problem outcomes" (p. xxviii). Protective factors can work in different ways, such as "shielding" a child from "experiencing a risk factor," reducing a child's "exposure to risk," and reducing "the impact of a risk factor" (Kids Matter, n.d., pp. 3–4). In addition, the National Association of Social Workers (NASW, n.d.) noted that protective factors have the ability to 1) serve as building blocks for developing resilience, 2) "protect and nurture adolescents in high risk situations," 3) "promote well-being," and 4) "reduce the likelihood of teenage suicide" (p. 1). Examples of protective factors against suicidal behaviors include connectedness to community or school (US Public Health Service, 1999), coping and problem-solving skills (Piquet & Wagner, 2003), family support (Perkins & Hartless, 2002), and positive self-concept or self-esteem (Fergusson et al., 2003).

Walsh and Eggert (2007) conducted a study that involved 730 US high school students who were experiencing school problems. These students were assessed for suicidal behaviors, risk factors, and protective factors. Based on data from the suicidal behavior assessment, students were divided into two subgroups: suicide risk (SR) and non-suicide risk (NSR). Data pertaining to risk and protective factors from the two subgroups (SR and NSR) were further analyzed. The statistical analysis revealed that SR youth reported significantly higher levels of risk factors pertaining to emotional distress (depression, anxiety, hopelessness, and anger) compared with NSR youth. Although no statistically significant difference in alcohol and marijuana use was found between the SR and NSR groups, a significantly higher level of other illicit drug use by the SR group was observed. Walsh and Eggert also reported that the "SR youth were significantly more likely than NSR youth to have engaged in high-risk behaviors, and to have reported witnessing or being a victim of violence" (p. 355). In regards to protective factors, SR youth reported significantly lower levels of all protective factors (self-esteem, personal control, problem-solving coping, amount of support, support availability, and family support satisfaction) compared with the NSR youth.

Walsh and Eggert (2007) recommended that an "examination of protective factors" be included in SR assessments (p. 357). This inclusion of protective factors in SR assessments has a great deal of potential and merits additional research. Although traditional suicide assessments tend to focus only on risk factors and levels of suicidal ideation, strengths-based suicide assessments acknowledge students' existing protective factors. The NASW (n.d.) stated that "targeting and eliminating risk factors may reduce the occurrence of suicide," and that prevention efforts are more effective when protective factors are strengthened concurrently while reducing risk factors (p. 2). To bolster protective factors, however, they must first be identified. The solution-focused approach is well suited for helping increase students' protective factors. Solution-focused school social workers assist clients in building their own capacity by focusing on the clients' strengths, coping skills, exceptions, and past successes. Due to the high number of students with mental health issues, it is not surprising that the solution-focused approach in school settings continues to grow in popularity because it is time limited, student focused, and strengths based.

How the Solution-Focused Approach Differs from Other Counseling Approaches

Most traditional counseling approaches focus efforts on discovering the explanations for *why* problems occur in order to resolve those problems (Birdsall & Miller, 2002). Unfortunately, uncovering the reasons why problems occur is not always helpful to students. For example, when the causes of problems are identified and/or highlighted, they are sometimes used by students as a "scapegoat to inhibit personal growth" or as reasons for why they cannot succeed (Sklare, 2005, p. 14). When students are dealing with multiple issues or experiencing suicidal ideation, they might become overwhelmed if therapeutic conversations focus primarily on their problems and the reasons for them. After hearing some of their personal stories, it is not surprising why some students feel even more hopeless or helpless, and why they shut down in counseling sessions. In addition to focusing on the reasons why problems occur, many counseling approaches such as cognitive-behavioral therapy (CBT) focus on "avoid goals" (Bannink, 2012, p. 14). For example, a traditional CBT school social worker might help a student develop avoid goals that involve the student identifying what he or she no longer wants in life, such as "I don't want to be depressed anymore."

The CBT school social worker often takes the role of an expert and makes recommendations about how the student could solve his or her problem(s).

On the other hand, a typical solution-focused school social worker would facilitate a conversation with the student and assist that student in developing "approach goals" (Bannink, 2012 p. 14). Approach goals are formed when a student describes the preferred future and what he or she wants in life, such as "I want to be happier" or "I want to make more friends." The solution-focused approach redirects attention and energy toward identifying what possible solutions may already exist instead of concentrating on problems. The inductive process incorporated within the solution-focused approach is similar to the trial-and-error method that students use to learn. Based on her experiences working with children, Insoo Kim Berg concluded that children do not need or want to know what caused their problems (Berg & Steiner, 2003). Instead, children would rather experiment to see what does and does not work for them. Use of the solution-focused approach in schools has been found to be effective because it is congruent with "how children think and view the world" (Berg & Steiner, 2003, p. xv). Its time-limited nature is especially useful for school-based mental health school social workers who might have large caseloads but not large amounts of time to work with students (Littrell, Malia, & Vanderwood, 1995). In addition, students are more likely to become engaged in a counseling session that focuses on their positive traits instead of their deficiencies (Sklare, 2005). Engaging students in the counseling process is especially important when working with students who are in crisis.

The Case of Brie and the Identification of Suicidal Ideation

Knowing how to recognize and respond to students' suicidal ideation is one of the biggest concerns and challenges for many school-based mental health school social workers. The following case study of Brie illustrates how the solution-focused approach may be used with a student who is experiencing suicidal ideation.

> Brie is a 16-year-old sophomore. Brie's mother has encouraged her to see Ms. Burns, a school social worker. Last year, Brie had worked with a different school-based mental health counselor who retired at the end of last year. Prior to their scheduled meeting, Ms. Burns had not worked with Brie. Although Brie has dealt with anxiety and depression in the past, she has become

more withdrawn and more resistant about going to school over the past couple of months. In addition, her grades have dropped significantly. Brie shuts down whenever her mom asks about why Brie doesn't want to go to school. Brie's mom is hoping Ms. Burns can find a way to get Brie to open up so that Brie can get the help she needs.

The following recommendations are used to help explain how Ms. Burns will approach her first session with Brie. These recommendations are also designed to be used with any student who is experiencing suicidal ideation. Although it is not discussed within the recommendations described below, please note that the solution-focused school social worker, Ms. Burns, has already gone through the informed consent process with Brie.

1. Develop Rapid Rapport with the Student by Using "Problem-Free Talk" at the Beginning of the Session

When working with a student who is in crisis, it is important to develop rapid rapport and find a way to join with the student (Berg, 1994). Fiske (2008) also pointed out that it is essential to get a client's attention in order to join with the student in the counseling process. She suggested that the solution-focused school social worker begin a session by focusing on "whatever is salient, relevant, and important" to the client (p. 7). This information could be discovered by using "problem-free talk" with the student (Henden, 2008, p. 77). Henden (2008) stressed that the first 10 minutes of a session are critical in the development of a counseling relationship. A student can either become engaged in the counseling process or begin to withdraw internally. It is imperative not to rush into talking about the student's problem before some level of rapport has been established. Without rapport, trust between the student and the solution-focused school social worker is difficult to develop. Conveying the core conditions of unconditional positive regard, empathy, and congruence can also have a significant impact on a counseling relationship (Rogers, 1951). Sharry, Darmody, and Madden (2002) noted that an effective solution-focused school social worker is one who "communicates empathic understanding, while also communicating a belief in the strengths of the client and in the possibility that they can make things different" (p. 387).

Because of the developmental stage they are in, some adolescents may be distrustful of adults when they begin the counseling process (Hopson &

Kim, 2004). It is helpful for solution-focused school social workers to be aware of this potential challenge when they work with students, especially adolescents. Fortunately, "solution-focused therapy is well-suited for work with adolescents in crisis because their stage of development may cause them to feel resentful of a more directive or problem-focused approach to therapy" (Hopson & Kim, 2004, p. 97). Henden (2008) noted that making a shift from a problem-focused conversation to a problem-free talk is a "great way to tap into the client's strengths, personal skills and resources before even the first detail of the problem is heard" (p. 77). Most solution-focused social workers will ask students about their interests, things they like to do, or activities/teams they are involved in both at and outside of school.

Here is an example of a problem-free question that can be used to elicit this useful information:

> Brie, what do you like to do in your free time when you are not in school?

For case students who are very depressed and state that they are no longer doing anything that they enjoy, the mental health school social worker could ask this follow-up question:

> So, before you started feeling really down, what did you used to do that you enjoyed?

Henden (2008) also discussed that problem-free talk can serve four different purposes: 1) It can normalize the interaction between the student and the mental health school social worker because "it is an even relationship; not 'one up'"; 2) it allows the solution-focused school social worker and the student to acknowledge the student's "strengths, skills, and resources"; 3) it "creates a context of competence" for the student because the focus is not on the student's challenges or problems; and 4) it provides an opportunity for the solution-focused school social worker to engage with the student, and not the student's problem (pp. 78–79). In addition, it is helpful to remember that problem-free talk is not small talk with a student. It is actually a valuable therapeutic tool used to increase client engagement.

2. Ask for a Brief Description of the Student's Concern

After initially engaging in problem-free talk with a student, a solution-focused school social worker may ask a student who has self-referred for counseling one of the following questions:

> Brie, what are you hoping that we can accomplish by working together?
> Brie, what were you hoping would happen when you asked to meet with me? (Hess, Magnuson, & Beeler, 2012)

By asking one of these questions, the school social worker is placed in a "not knowing" position, which may help to counter any preconceptions that might arise about the student's situation and what the student might need from school social worker (De Jong & Berg, 2008, p. 215). To clarify the student's primary concern, the solution-focused school social worker can ask follow-up questions such as:

> What concerns you most about this situation?
> What is the hardest part of this for you? (Hess et al., 2012, p. 150)

If a student was referred to counseling by someone else, such a teacher or a parent/guardian, the school social worker may need to approach these initial questions a little differently. For example, the solution-focused school social worker could ask the student:

> What do you think [person who referred the student] is hoping that you and I accomplish by working together?

Students who are referred by other people may be more reluctant to engage in the counseling process or voluntarily share information, which is understandable, especially since these students were not the ones who initially asked for help. Solution-focused school social workers strive to be respectfully curious when working with students. One simple way of demonstrating respect to a student is simply by asking the student for permission to ask a question, especially if asking about a sensitive topic. For example, a solution-focused school social worker could ask:

> Brie, would it be okay if I asked you about . . . ?

Although this question might seem redundant and simplistic, it actually conveys a great deal of respect because some students may view unsolicited questions from mental health school social workers as very intrusive. In addition to demonstrating respect for the student, this question may help to develop a strong therapeutic relationship.

To encourage the student to give a brief problem description, the school social worker could ask:

> Brie, what would be most helpful for me to know about your situation?

This question is also respectful because it allows the student to decide what information he or she feels is most important for the mental health school social worker to know. When working with clients who had experienced trauma, Dolan (1991) would ask them disclose "only what was necessary for healing" (p. 142). It is important that students feel like they still retain substantial control over the content of information shared in counseling sessions. In addition, solution-focused school social workers need to convey to their clients that they are interested in identifying what would immediately benefit the student, not in identifying and focusing on the causes of their problems (Fiske, 2008). When solution-focused school social workers are successful in communicating this, they are more likely to see clients who 1) open up more freely, 2) engage in the counseling process, and 3) return for follow-up sessions if they need additional assistance (Fiske, 2008).

Henden (2008) noted that some critics of the solution-focused approach believe that solution-focused school social workers "are not interested in hearing about problems" (p. 80). Henden countered this criticism by stating that solution-focused school social workers do spend time listening to clients' problems. In fact, Sharry et al. (2002) stated that the solution-focused approach "is not problem or pain phobic" (p. 387). Furthermore, "clients need to feel that their problems and difficulties are taken seriously, that their suffering is acknowledged and that they are not blamed for the problem" (Sharry et al., p. 387). Solution-focused school social workers also realize, however, that too much time spent focusing exclusively on client problems can be counterproductive for students (Henden, 2008). In addition, Henden (2008) commented that clients will return to "problem talk" if they felt that their mental health school social workers had heard enough about their problems (p. 105). Sharry et al. (2002) also recommended that while a client is describing his or her problems, a solution-focused school social worker should actively listen for the strengths and coping skills that the client has already used.

3. Assess for Incongruence

Although some students may provide verbal and non-verbal communication that clearly indicates they are experiencing suicidal ideation, others may not provide congruent information. In addition, it is possible for a student with suicidal ideation to initially tell a school social worker that he or she is not suicidal when asked a direct question about such ideation. Therefore, it is recommended that a solution-focused school social worker simultaneously assess for any incongruences between the student's verbal and non-verbal communication while the student is describing his or her problem (Henden, 2008). Incongruence may be a warning sign that the student is dealing with suicidal ideation that has not been explicitly expressed to the school social worker.

4. Ask Questions Designed to Elicit Suicidal Ideation if Present

When a solution-focused school social worker has concerns (even if just be at a gut-feeling level) that a student might be experiencing suicidal ideation, the social worker needs to ask one or two questions designed to elicit any hidden suicidal ideation that the student is experiencing. For example:

> Brie, I'm sensing that you are going through a really tough time right now. Am I understanding your situation correctly?

If the student expresses that he or she is, in fact, going through a difficult time, it is helpful for the solution-focused school social worker to ask a scaling question to quickly assess the situation. For example:

> Brie, on a scale of 1 to 10, with 1 being not well at all and 10 being very well, how well do you feel right now as you are talking with me?

If the student then indicates that he or she is not doing well, or if the solution-focused school social worker senses that the student may have deeper concerns, the social worker could ask the student one of the following questions for clarification:

> Brie, on a scale of 1 to 10, with 1 being close and 10 being not close at all, how close do you feel right now to ending your life?

Brie, on a scale of 1 to 10, with 1 being very suicidal and 10 being not suicidal at all, how suicidal do you feel right now?

It is surprising how honest many students are about revealing their suicidal ideation when asked a scaling question. Since some students may struggle to choose descriptive words to convey their personal pain, they may find it easier to use a number on a scale to represent how they are feeling. This basic number can provide a great deal of information and even help prompt a meaningful conversation between the student and the mental health school social worker.

5. Engage the Student in a "Coping Dialogue" if the Student Is Not Ready to Start the Goal Formation Process

De Jong and Berg (2008) stressed that after suicidal ideation has been identified, the solution-focused school social worker needs to get a sense of whether a client has the "immediate capacity" to move into the goal formation process (p. 233). In addition, they pointed out that "the major difference in working with clients in crisis is that fewer of them accept the invitation to engage in goal formation" (p. 233). Instead of jumping into the goal formation and solution-building process, some clients in crisis seem more entrenched in focusing on their problems. As a result, De Jong and Berg recommended that in these cases, solution-focused school social workers put the goal formation process on hold and shift their attention to asking their clients coping questions. When the timing is appropriate, solution-focused school social workers can shift back to the solution-building process.

Coping questions help "uncover small, undeniable successes that a shaken, overwhelmed client is experiences in day-to-day or moment-by-moment coping" (De Jong & Berg, 2008, p. 233). For example, a solution-focused school social worker might highlight a student's small coping success by asking:

> Brie, I have question you. What helped you get out of bed this morning so that you could make it to school on time and we could meet together today?

De Jong and Berg (2008) stressed the importance of identifying a client's "microsuccesses," especially when the client might be extremely overwhelmed or feeling very defeated (p. 233). These microsuccesses build over time, which in turn can help increase a client's confidence and energy level.

Solution-Focused Brief Therapy in Schools

Once the client's confidence and energy have increased a little, the school social worker can return "to goal formation on a more limited basis by using scaling questions to help clients formulate their next steps in coping" (p. 233). Fiske (2008) also pointed out that an important role of solution-focused school social workers is to help their clients "develop longer lists of coping strategies, including more life-affirming alternatives" (p. 157)

The following coping questions and statements have been slightly modified from Henden's (2008) original versions. These questions are presuppositional in nature and designed to help build on hope. In addition, they are designed to be empowering and affirming of the student. An opening question could be:

> Brie, tell me about a time in the last couple of weeks when you felt the least suicidal.

This question can be used as a lead-in for asking coping questions such as the following:

> Brie, what has stopped you from ending your life up to this point in time?

This question is designed to identify possible reasons for living. Fiske (2008) stated that "identifying, highlighting, and reinforcing reasons for living is key to engaging in helpful conversations with individuals who are viewing suicide as a solution to their problems" (p. 8). The solution-focused school social worker may also ask:

> Brie, what have you done in the last couple of weeks that has made a positive difference on dealing with your tough situation?

If the student shares with the solution-focused school social worker that he or she has experienced suicidal ideation in the past, the solution-focused school social worker could ask the student the following coping question:

> Brie, what did you do back then when you had suicidal ideation that helped you make it through that difficult time?

This coping question encourages the student to explore coping skills that he or she already possesses and to identify times when the student successfully

---

dealt with a difficult period (in other words, highlighting a "past success"). The solution-focused school social worker might also ask a scaling question designed to elicit information about the student's current coping ability such as:

> Brie, on a scale of 1 to 10, with 1 being very weak and 10 being very strong, how strong do you think your coping skills are now as you are talking with me?

This coping question is very important because the solution-focused school social worker can use it to encourage students to self-evaluate whether they feel capable of using their current resources (coping skills) or need additional resources. De Jong and Berg (2008) stated that "if you have engaged a client in a coping dialogue and the dialogue reveals few if any current coping capacities, the client often comes to realize that he or she needs more intensive care and monitoring" (p. 233). Student who come to their own realization that additional help is needed may be more likely to accept help and engage in the solution-building process.

In traditional suicidal ideation assessment, great emphasis is placed on the problem assessment, which is designed to get as many details about the student's suicidal ideation as possible. For example, a CBT school social worker might use a common suicide assessment acronym PLAID (Plan, Lethal means, Attempts, Intent, Drugs/alcohol) to formulate questions for the student (Granello & Granello, 2007, p. 47). Gathering these details is often the main focus of the conversation between the traditional school social worker and the student. As discussed earlier, and in contrast, solution-focused school social workers spend more time focusing on students' coping skills and strengths instead gathering a detailed description of the problem. Sometimes, however, a solution-focused school social worker may need to gather more detailed information about a problem. In those cases, the solution-focused school social worker might ask:

> Brie, if you decided to go ahead with the option to end your life,. . .
> a. How prepared are you if you decided to do this? (This question could also be turned into a scaling question.)
> b. What method would you use? (Henden, 2008, p. 129)

Ironically, students are likely to share more information about their problems during coping dialogues than during formal problem assessments.

De Jong and Berg (2008) strongly believed that the best chance for helping clients/students who are experiencing suicidal ideation is to "mobilize their strengths and reestablish a sense of control over their emotions and circumstances" by asking "coping questions" and by encouraging the students to "amplify their answers" (p. 224).

6. Acknowledge, Validate, and Normalize a Student's Feelings

If a student's suicidal ideation has been identified, it is important to acknowledge, validate, and normalize the student's feelings.

Acknowledge

Henden (2008) believed clients who are suicidal have an "intuitive radar" and can detect whether a mental health school social worker is being "genuine, and has some degree of appreciation of their pain and suffering" (p. 91). It could also be argued that many adolescents by nature are very perceptive and can sense if adults are being sincere. Therefore, it is very important for the school social worker to acknowledge the adolescent's pain in an authentic manner. For example, the solution-focused school social worker could state:

> Brie, from what you've told me about your situation at home, you have given me a pretty good idea about how difficult it is for you right now.

By their problems acknowledged, student are more likely to feel understood by the solution-focused school social worker and engage in a therapeutic relationship (Henden, 2008).

Validate

In addition to acknowledging students' pain and challenges, it is important to validate their feelings and their suicidal thoughts. De Jong and Berg (2008) noted that the first impulse of some beginning school social workers is to try convincing suicidal clients that "suicide is illogical, dangerous, and hurtful to others, or an otherwise distorted response to their situation" (p. 223). Unfortunately, taking this approach with a student who is suicidal may unintentionally increase the risk of suicide (Henden, 2008). By refuting or challenging the student's ideas, the school social worker may cause the student to feel even more isolated, which obviously has a negative impact the therapeutic relationship (De Jong & Berg, 2008). Adolescents may already be distrustful of adults, so invalidating their perceptions could have potentially serious consequences.

A traditional school social worker might be tempted to ask:

> Brie, why would you consider suicide when you have so much to live for?

However, asking students "Why" they did (or are doing) something can often put students on the defensive and shut them down from sharing more information. In addition, "Why" questions inadvertently convey that a judgment is being made by the school social worker (Sharry et al., 2002). Instead, a solution-focused school social worker finds it more productive to validate a student's thoughts or actions by stating:

> Brie, based on everything that you've shared with me, it's understandable that you are having some suicidal thoughts.

By validating and viewing a student's suicidal ideation as an *attempt* to find a solution to an overwhelming problem, the solution-focused school social worker strives to reduce the student's feelings of shame or inadequacy about his or her coping skills (Hawkes, Marsh, & Wilgosh, 1998). In addition, the solution-focused school social worker hopes to engage the client in a collaborative process of identifying more effective coping methods that the client has used in the past.

Normalize

Henden (2008) noted that "many suicidal clients express the view that, as a result of having suicidal thoughts and ideas, they must be going mad" (p. 92). Normalizing a student's suicidal ideation or feelings is an important part of helping someone who might also be feeling that he or she is losing control over life or his or her mind. Henden (2008) provided this helpful example of how to normalize a student's suicidal ideation:

> Most people who are feeling trapped or defeated by a challenging situation in their lives, have suicidal thoughts from time to time. It is a normal response, by normal people, to abnormal set of circumstances. (p. 92)

These powerful words could be very comforting and affirming to a client who might be afraid to seek assistance in coping with suicidal ideation.

7. Assist the Student with the Goal Formation Process

Remember that students who are suicidal or in crisis build solutions through the same process used by other clients (De Jong & Berg, 2008). As noted earlier, however, a coping dialogue may need to take place before a suicidal student is ready to move into the goal formation process. When it is time to start developing goals, solution-focused school social workers commonly ask a miracle question. But the typical miracle question often used to help form goals with students who are not in crisis may need to be adapted for students who are experiencing suicidal ideation.

Henden (2008) recommended the miracle question be "adapted in such a way that the exclusion of suicidal thoughts and feelings is the miracle" (p. 141). Here is an example based on Henden's (2008) suggestion:

> Let's suppose that while you are sleeping in your bed tonight, a miracle happens. The miracle is that all of your suicidal thoughts and feelings are gone. However, you don't know this miracle has taken place because you were sleeping. When you wake up the next morning, what would be the first sign to you that this miracle happened?

After asking this miracle question, the solution-focused school social worker tries to get as many details as possible about what the student is *doing*. The richness of these details will provide valuable information that can be used to assist the client in developing his or her "SMART+" goals ("small, measureable, achievable, realistic, and time limited"), which also include the presence of "some positive behavior, rather than the absence of negative behaviors" (Henden, 2008, p. 81). For example, the solution-focused school social worker could ask:

> Brie, what would you be doing? ... What else? ... Okay, and what else?

The focus here is on identifying the student's positive behaviors and actions. It is also helpful to ask a relationship question such as:

> Brie, what would other people notice you doing?

By asking a relationship question that encourages the student to view things from a third-person perspective, it may be easier for the student to provide richer details and ideas that can in turn be used to help develop goals.

When solution-focused school social workers use the miracle question to shift the focus to what a student wants or is trying to achieve through suicide, the school social worker subtly encourages the student to evaluate if suicide is the best alternative to getting it. De Jong and Berg (2008) also recommended tailoring the miracle question to fit each client's situation. They explained that "it is important to scale down the miracle" if the client had experienced a "major disruption" in his or her life (De Jong & Berg, 2008, p. 220). For example, the miracle might involve the student being able to sleep a little better or make it to school on time.

After collaborating with the student to set a goal, it is helpful to ask a scaling question to assess the student's motivation or confidence about completing his/her goal. For example:

> Brie, on a scale of 1 to 10, with 1 being not confident at all and 10 being extremely confident, how confident are you about achieving this goal?

This question can easily be modified to ask the student how "motivated" he or she is to accomplishing the identified goal.

8. Encourage the Student to Go Slow and Take Very Small Steps

Sharry et al. (2002) explained that developing goals with clients "who have felt so immersed in their problems that they attempted suicide" can be challenging and may take time (p. 392). The solution-focused school social worker needs to take things slow, however, and look for other ways of encouraging students to develop positive goals. Metcalf (1995) also noted that "change takes time" and that "the best changes occur over time" (p. 86). As a result, she encouraged students to "take small steps" (p. 86). Furthermore, Metcalf recommended that solution-focused school social workers caution their students to go slowly through the counseling process. With this caution in mind, students might be less likely to perceive their slow progress as a failure. Henden (2008) also described the importance of encouraging clients to take "small steps or 'baby steps'" in counseling (p. 148). When working with clients who are suicidal or in crisis, Henden adapted this recommendation by encouraging clients to take "very, very small steps" (p. 148).

9. Assist the Student in Identifying Exceptions

One important task of the solution-focused school social worker is to work collaboratively with a student to "tap into hope" (Fiske, 2008, p. 16). Since hopelessness is a major risk factor for suicidal behavior, building hope within a student dealing with suicidal ideation is even more imperative (Csorba et al., 2003; Perkins & Hartless, 2002). A basic assumption of the solution-focused approach is that no problem is constant and the intensity of the problem fluctuates (Murphy, 1997). One effective method for tapping into hope and building upon it is to aid students in identifying exceptions (times when the problem is not occurring, is less frequent, or less severe).

Hendon (2008) noted that it is helpful to look for exceptions after information is gathered by asking a miracle question. For example:

> Brie, I'm curious to know if a small part of your miracle has happened, or if a small part of it is happening today. Tell me more about the last time you felt a little better.
>
> So, Brie, I'm curious about the last time you were feeling a little less suicidal. What were you doing (or thinking) differently than you are today?

Follow-up questions may include:

> How did you make that happen? ... What else? ... Okay, and what else?
> How did you decide to do that?
> What did you discover by doing that?
> What would happen if you tried that again?

Other options of exception-finding questions include:

> What was different about the time you were in emotional crisis but did not consider suicide as an option? (Fiske, 2008, p. 46)
> What is different about those times that you are not thinking about suicide? (Fiske, 2008, p. 46)

Follow-up questions amplify the exceptions. Murphy (1994) described the 5-E method, which was designed to recognize and use exceptions that exist in students' lives. Solution-focused school social workers using the 5-E method can assist students to 1) elicit times when the problem is absent, less intense, or less frequent; 2) elaborate on the conditions and features of these

---

times; 3) expand these identified exceptions to other contexts; 4) evaluate these exceptions using pre-established goals; and 5) empower the client to maintain positive change over time (Murphy, 1994). Since exceptions are often overlooked, solution-focused school social workers need to be very intentional in identifying and amplifying these "microsolutions" (Sharry et al., 2002, p. 392).

10. Compliment the Student

Complimenting students is an effective method for highlighting and reinforcing students' strengths and resources. Remember, however, that solution-focused compliments should be based in reality and are not given just to be "nice" or "kind." There are also different forms of solution-focused compliments, such as direct verbal compliments and indirect verbal compliments (Fiske, 2008). A direct verbal compliment is a positive reaction or evaluation by the solution-focused school social worker in response to what the student has shared in a session. For example:

> Wow, Brie! I'm sure that must have been difficult for you to confront your friend about her hurtful comments and yet your found the courage to do it.

An indirect compliment involves inviting the student through the use of a question to describe what the student did and what worked well for the student. For example:

> Wow, Brie, how did you manage to get the courage to confront your friend about her hurtful comments?
> What did your friend notice that you did well in how you approached this situation?

Both types of compliments encourage students to reflect on their own competence. In addition, they may result in students giving a self-compliment when explaining how and what they did to make things happen.

Compliments that are given near the end of a session can also get a student's attention and encouraging the student to become more receptive to carrying out therapeutic tasks after the session (Henden, 2008). For example:

> Brie, a couple of things that really stand out to me from our conversation today is how determined you are to feel better and

how willing you were to share some of your coping mechanisms with me. I'm impressed by your actions especially since I know it isn't easy for you to open up to adults.

II. Provide Bridging Statements, and Identify Tasks

After the solution-focused school social worker has given compliments and begins the process of wrapping up the session, he or she will use bridging statements that link to therapeutic tasks. Henden (2008) noted that a "bridging statement at the end of a particular session is most likely to refer to something which has arisen during the session that can be used as a small step in their homework before the next session." (p. 101). For example:

> Brie, today you mentioned that you felt a little better when you volunteered at your grandmother's nursing home. Would you be interested in having arrangements made for you to spend some more time helping out there again?

If it is the first session in which a student's suicidal ideation has been identified, it is also important to notify the student's parent/guardian about the suicidal ideation. In this situation, a bridging statement could be used to involve the student in helping with this notification. For example:

> Brie, at the beginning of our session, we discussed confidentiality and the reasons for when I need to break it. Well, I'm sure it won't come as a surprise when I say that we need to let your mom know about your suicidal ideation. It is really important that you are safe. I want make sure we provide you some additional support since you are experiencing a lot of strong emotions right now. How would you prefer to contact your mom? Would you like to call your mom in my office right now, or would you like me to call your mom while you are here with me?

Although the school social worker tells Brie that they need to contact her mom, the school social worker still gives Brie the choice on how to do this. During the conversation with Brie's mom, the school social worker not only shares Brie's suicidal ideation but also emphasizes Brie's coping skills and exceptions when things have gone a little better for her.

12. Wrap Up the Session

After the conversation with Brie's mom, the school social worker (Ms. Burns) makes a point of wrapping up the session. Part of this summary includes highlighting Brie's current coping skills and her ability to deal with challenging times in the past. The school social worker also confirms with Brie possible therapeutic tasks that she plans to complete. The session wrap-up is an important part of the counseling process and should not be overlooked. The severity of Brie's suicidal ideation will determine whether she will need outside assistance or will continue working with Ms. Burns in the school. Either way, this initial solution-focused counseling session is designed to build hope, to empower Brie, and to encourage further solution-building activities.

Conclusion

> "The wise person doesn't give the right answers, instead the wise person poses the right questions."

This adapted quote by French anthropologist, Claude Levi-Strauss, does a wonderful job of summarizing the inherent value of the solution-focused approach. Solution-focused school social workers are not the experts of their students' lives, nor are they required to provide all the right answers even when working with students who are experiencing crises. Instead, solution-focused school social workers are fortunate to have access to a wide array of powerful and effective therapeutic questions that can be used during the collaborative solution-building process with their students. In addition, the solution-focused approach helps facilitate the "hope-building" process that is so important when working with students who are struggling or are feeling hopeless.

Henden (2008) posed some important questions to mental health school social workers when he asked:

> Is it not better to look on hope, rather than despair? Is it not better to ask questions about what is working, rather than what is not? And, is it not better to empower people to take steps towards building their own solutions to their difficulties, rather than trying to do things unto them? (p. 196)

After reviewing solution-focused research and literature, it would be hard not to answer a strong "Yes" to all three of his questions.

References

Bannink, F. (2012). *Practicing positive CBT: From reducing distress to building success.* Hoboken, NJ: Wiley-Blackwell.

Berg, I. K. (1994). *Family-based services: A solution-focused approach.* New York, NY: Norton.

Berg, I. K., & Steiner, T. (2003). *Children's solution work.* New York, NY: Norton.

Bernard, B. (1991). Fostering resiliency in kids. *Educational Leadership, 51*(3), 44–48.

Beautrais, A. L. (2001). Child and young adolescent suicide in New Zealand. *Australian and New Zealand Journal of Psychiatry, 35,* 647–653.

Birdsall, B. A., & Miller, L. D. (2002). Brief counseling in schools: A solution-focused approach for school counselors. *Counseling and Human Development, 35*(2), 1–10.

Breton, J., Tousignant, M., Bergeron, L., & Berthiaume, C. (2002). Informant-specific correlates of suicidal behavior in a community survey of 12- to 14-year-olds. *Journal of the American Academy of Child and Adolescent Psychiatry, 38,* 723–730.

Brown, J., Cohen, P., Johnson, J. G., & Smailes, E. M. (1999). Childhood abuse and neglect: Specificity of effects on adolescent and young adult depression and suicidality. *Journal of the American Academy of Child and Adolescent Psychiatry, 38,* 1490–1496.

Centers for Disease Control and Prevention (CDC). (2013, May 17). Mental health surveillance among children—United States, 2005–2011. *MMWR Morbidity and Mortality Weekly Report, 62*(2), Supplement. Retrieved from http://www.cdc.gov/mmwr/pdf/other/su6202.pdf

Centers for Disease Control and Prevention (CDC). (n.d.-a). *10 Leading causes of death by age group, United States—2013.* Retrieved from http://www.cdc.gov/injury/wisqars/pdf/leading_causes_of_death_by_age_group_2013-a.pdf

Centers for Disease Control and Prevention (CDC). (n.d.-b). *10 Leading causes of death by age group, United States—2010.* Retrieved from http://www.cdc.gov/injury/wisqars/pdf/10LCID_All_Deaths_By_Age_Group_2010-a.pdf

Centers for Disease Control and Prevention (CDC). (n.d.-c). *Trends in the prevalence of suicide–related behavior national YRBS: 1991–2013.* Retrieved from http://www.cdc.gov/healthyyouth/yrbs/pdf/trends/us_suicide_trend_yrbs.pdf

Congress.gov. (2015a). *H.R. 1211—Mental health in schools act of 2015.* Retrieved from https://www.congress.gov/bill/114th-congress/house-bill/1211

Congress.gov. (2015b). *S. 1588—Mental health in schools act of 2015.* Retrieved from https://www.congress.gov/bill/114th-congress/senate-bill/1588

Csorba, J., Rozsa, S., Gadoros, J., Vetro, A., Kaczinszky, A., Sarungi, E., Makra, J., & Kapornay, K. (2003). Suicidal depressed vs. non-suicidal depressed adolescents: Differences in recent psychopathology. *Journal of Affective Disorders, 74,* 229–236.

De Jong, P., & Berg, I. K. (2008). *Interviewing for solutions* (3rd ed.). Belmont, CA: Thomson.

Dolan, Y. (1991). *Resolving sexual abuse: Solution-focused therapy and Ericksonian hypnosis for adult survivors.* New York, NY: Norton.

Erford, B. T., Newsome, D. W., & Rock, E. (2007). Counseling youth at risk. In B. T. Erford (Ed.) *Transforming the school counseling profession* (2nd ed., pp. 279–303). Upper Saddle River, NJ: Pearson.

Fergusson, D. M., Beautrais, A. L., & Horwood, L. J. (2003). Vulnerability and resiliency to suicidal behaviors in young people. *Psychological Medicine, 33*, 61–73.

Friedman, R. M., Katz-Levey, J. W., Manderschied, R. W., & Sondheimer, D. L. (1996b). Prevalence of serious emotional disturbance in children and adolescents. In R. W. Manderscheid & M. A. Sonnenschein (Eds.), *Mental health, United States, 1996* (pp. 71–88). Rockville, MD: Center for Mental Health Services.

Fiske, H. (2008). *Hope in action: Solution-focused conversations about suicide.* New York, NY: Routledge.

Galassi, J. P., & Akos, P. (2007). *Strengths-based school counseling: Promoting student development and achievement.* Mahwah, NJ: Lawrence Erlbaum.

Granello, D., & Granello, P. (2007) Suicide assessment: Strategies for determining risk. *Counselling, Psychotherapy, and Health, 3(1),* 42–51.

Gray, D., Achilles, J., Keller, T., Tate, D., Haggard, L., Rolfs, R., Cazier, C., Workman, J., & McMahaon, W. M. (2002). Utah youth suicide study, phase I: Government agency contact before death. *Journal of the American Academy of Child and Adolescent Psychiatry, 41*, 427–434.

Groholt, B., Ekeberg, O., Wichstrom, L., & Haldorsen, T. (2000). Young suicide attempters: A comparison between a clinical and an epidemiological sample. *Journal of the American Academy of Child and Adolescent Psychiatry, 39*, 868–875.

Hawkes, D., Marsh, T. I., & Wilgosh, R. (1998). *Solution-focused therapy: A handbook for health care professionals.* Boston, MA: Butterworth-Heinemann

Henden, J. (2008). *Preventing suicide: The solution-focused approach.* West Sussex, UK: Wiley.

Hess, R. S., Magnuson, S., & Beeler, L. (2012). *Counseling children and adolescents in school.* Los Angeles, CA: Sage.

Hoagwood, K., & Erwin, H. (1997) Effectiveness of school-based mental health services for children: A 10-year research review. *Journal of Child and Family Studies, 6*, 435–451.

Hopson, L. M., & Kim, J. S. (2004). A solution-focused approach to crisis intervention with adolescent. *Journal of Evidence-Based Social Work, 1*(2-3): 93–110. doi:10.1300/J394v01n02_07

Kids Matter. (n.d.). *Mental health risk and protective factors.* Retrieved from https://www.kidsmatter.edu.au/sites/default/files/public/KMP_C3_RPFCMH_MentalHealthRiskAndProtectiveFactors.pdf

King, R. A., Schwab-Stone, M., Flisher, A. J., Greenwald, S., Kramer, R. A., Goodman, S. H., Lahey, B. B., Shaffer, D., & Gould, M. S. (2001). Psychosocial and risk behavior correlates of youth suicide attempts and suicide ideation. *Journal of the American Academy of Child and Adolescent Psychiatry, 40*, 837–847.

Littrell, J., Malia, J., & Vanderwood, M. (1995). Single-session brief counseling in a high school. *Journal of Counseling and Development, 73*, 451–458.

Massachusetts Executive Office of Health and Human Services (MEOHHS). (n.d.). *Risk & protective factors.* Retrieved from http://www.mass.gov/eohhs/gov/departments/dph/programs/substance-abuse/providers/prevention/risk-and-protective-factors.html

---

Merikangas, K. R., He, J., Burstein, M., Swanson, S. A., Avenevoli, S., Cui, L., Benjet, C., Georgiades, K., & Swendsen, J. (2010). Lifetime prevalence of mental disorders in US adolescents: Results from the National Comorbidity Survey Replication–Adolescent Supplement (NCS-A). *Journal of American Academy of Child and Adolescent Psychiatry, 40*(10), 980–989.

Metcalf, L. (1995). *Counseling toward solutions: A practical solution-focused program for working with students, teachers, and parents.* San Francisco, CA: Jossey-Bass.

Murphey, D., Barry, M., & Vaugh, B. (2013, January). *Positive mental health: Resilience.* Publication 2013-3. Retrieved from http://www.childtrends.org/wp-content/uploads/2013/03/Child_Trends-2013_11_01_AHH_Resilience.pdf

Murphy, J. J. (1994). Working with what works: A solution-focused approach to school behavior problems. *School Counselor, 42*, 59–68.

Murphy, J. J. (1997). *Solution-focused counseling in middle and high schools.* Alexandria, VA: American Counseling Association.

National Alliance on Mental Illness (NAMI). (2014). *State mental health legislation 2014: Trends, themes & effective practices.* Retrieved from https://www.nami.org/legreport2014

National Association of Social Workers (NASW). (n.d.). *School social workers' role in addressing students' mental health needs and increasing academic achievement.* Retrieved from https://www.socialworkers.org/practice/adolescent_health/shift/documents/information/SHIFT-Protective.pdf

O'Connell, M. E., Boat, T., & Warner, K. E. (eds.) (2009). *Preventing mental, emotional, and behavioral disorders among young people: Progress and possibilities.* Washington, DC: National Academies Press.

Perkins, D. F., & Hartless, G. (2002). An ecological risk-factor examination of suicidal ideation and behavior in adolescents. *Journal of Adolescent Research, 17*, 3–26.

Piquet, M. L., & Wagner, B. M. (2003). Coping responses of adolescent suicide attempters and their relation to suicide ideation across a 2-year follow-up: A preliminary study. *Suicide and Life-Threatening Behaviour, 33*, 288–301.

Rak, C. F., & Patterson, L. E. (1996). Promoting resilience in at-risk children. *Journal of Counseling & Development, 74*, 368–373.

Rogers, C. R. (1951). *Client-centered therapy.* Boston, MA: Houghton Mifflin.

Ruchkin, V. V., Schwab-Stone, M., Koposov, R. A., Vermeiren, R., & King, R. A. (2003). Suicidal ideations and attempts in juvenile delinquents. *Journal of Child Psychology and Psychiatry, 44*, 1058–1066.

Sharry, J., Darmody, M., & Madden, B. (2002). A solution-focused approach to working with clients who are suicidal. *British Journal of Guidance & Counselling, 30*(4), 383–399.

Sklare, G. B. (2005). *Brief counseling that works: A solution-focused approach for school counselors and administrators* (2nd ed.). Thousand Oaks, CA: Corwin Press.

US Public Health Service. (1999). *Mental Health: A Report of the Surgeon General.* Washington, DC: U.S. Department of Health and Human Services.

US Department of Health and Human Services. (2014). *Youth risk behavior surveillance-United States, 2013.* Retrieved from https://www.cdc.gov/mmwr/pdf/ss/ss6304.pdf

US Department of Health and Human Services. (1999). *Mental health: A report of the Surgeon General*. Rockville, MD: Center for Mental Health Services.

Walrath, C. M., Mandell, D. S., Liao, Q., Holden, E. W., De Carolis, G., Santiago, R. L., & Leaf, P. J. (2001). Suicide attempts in the "Comprehensive Community Mental Health Services for Children and Their Families" program. *Journal of the American Academy of Child and Adolescent Psychiatry, 40*, 1197–1205.

Walsh, E., & Eggert, L. L. (2007). Suicide risk and protective factors among youth experiencing school difficulties. *International Journal of Mental Health Nursing, 16*(5), 349–359.

Werner, E. E., & Smith, R. S. (1992). *Overcoming the odds: High risk children from birth to adulthood*. Ithaca, NY: Cornell University Press.

Wichstrom, L. (2000). Predictors of adolescent suicide attempts: A nationally representative longitudinal study of Norwegian adolescents. *Journal of the American Academy of Child and Adolescent Psychiatry, 39*, 603–610.

9

SFBT in Action
Substance Use
Adam S. Froerer & Elliott E. Connie

Overview of Substance Abuse Nationally and in Schools

Substance use is common among teens and adults, and this issue continually impacts laws as well as school policies and procedures. School officials and mental health professionals working within school settings frequently encounter substance use among students. Young people may use for purposes, experimentation, or more seriously and/or because of dependence. Although the prevalence rates for adolescent substance use overall have decreased slightly in the past few years, as many as 14.2% of adolescents between the ages of 12 and 17 are still reporting some substance use within the past month of being surveyed (US Department of Health and Human Services, 2013). This significant value indicates that both school officials and mental health professionals will likely interact with students who are actively using or have recently used substances. This chapter explains one effective approach, SFBT, to working with these substance-using students.

Definitions

The US Department of Health and Human Services (2008) advocates that professionals view substance involvement on a continuum with six anchor points: 1) abstinence, 2) use, 3) abuse, 4) abuse/dependence, 5) recovery, and 6) secondary abstinence. *Abstinence* means to refrain from using. In the case of substance use, it means to refrain from using alcohol and/or drugs. *Use* involves minimal use of substances and generally results in few and/or minimal consequences. *Abuse* occurs with regular use and results in consequences that become more significant and severe. *Abuse/dependence* is regular use over a sustained period of time and results in physical dependence and accompanying withdrawal symptoms. *Recovery* is returning to a state of abstinence. *Secondary abstinence* is returning to abstinence after relapse. In addition, *experimentation* is when an individual tries something new or uses for the first time. Experimentation is generally undertaken to have a new experience.

These definitions are complemented by the new conceptualization within the fifth edition of the *Diagnostic and Statistical Manual of Mental Disorders* (DSM-5). The DSM-5 no longer uses categories or diagnoses of substance abuse and substance dependence. Now, these disorders are classified as substance use disorders and can be further specified by which substance the individual is using (e. g., Alcohol Use Disorder or Marijuana Use Disorder). In addition, classifiers (mild, moderate, or severe) are added to the diagnosis to indicate the level of severity; these classifiers are determined by the number of diagnostic criteria the individual meets. Some symptom indicators taken into consideration for diagnostic purposes are 1) level of recurrent use, 2) amount or severity of impairment, 3) potential health problems related to substance use, 4) disability, and/or 5) failure to meet major responsibilities at work, school or at home. Overall, substance use disorders are determined based on evidence of impaired control, social impairment, risk of use, and pharmacological criteria. Holding this view of use should help to inform school social workers regarding appropriate assessment and treatment options and appropriate intervention strategies.

Prevalence Rates of Substance Use Among School-Aged Persons

Adolescents report having used many different substances, including alcohol, anabolic steroids, bath salts, cocaine, ecstasy, GHB, hallucinogens, heroin, inhalants, ketamine, marijuana, methamphetamine, nicotine, opioids, over-the-counter drugs, PCP, pain relievers, prescription medication, Rohypnol, stimulants, synthetic cannabis, and tobacco, among others. Table 9.1 outlines the 2013 data (most recent available) regarding substance use for adolescents (9th–12th graders) according to the National Youth Risk Behavior Study conducted by the Centers of Disease Control and Prevention.

Although usage rates have decreased since 2011, with the exception of marijuana use (and most not statistically significantly lower), a significant proportion of teenagers have used drugs/alcohol sometime in their lives

Table 9.1 Adolescent Substance Use Percentages

Substance	Ever Used in Percent (2011 statistics)
Marijuana	40.7 (39.9)
Cocaine	5.5 (6.8)
Hallucinogenic drugs	7.1 (8.7)
Inhalants	8.9 (11.4)
Heroin	2.2 (2.9)
Methamphetamines	3.2 (3.8)
Alcohol	66.2 (70.8)
Tobacco	41.1 (44.7)

(Office of Applied Studies, 2013). If we look closer at alcohol use (the highest prevalence rate), 35% of teenager surveyed reported drinking "some amount of alcohol" during the past 30 days, with 21% reporting they had at least one episode of binge drinking within the past 30 days and 10% reported having driven after drinking. In addition to the substances listed in Table 9.1, it should be noted that 2.2% of school-aged teens also reported non-medical use of prescription-type drugs, and one in eight teens reported that they were approached by someone selling drugs in the past month of being surveyed.

These statistics do not provide an exhaustive overview of the current state of adolescent substance use, and we acknowledge that the numbers could be inaccurate due to the reliance on self-reporting. These numbers do, however, highlight that many adolescents have used drugs/alcohol, are currently using substances, or are at risk for future substance use. It is vital for school personnel and mental health professionals to be aware of these statistics (and more importantly, the individuals at risk represented by these statistics) and the risk/protective factors for our youth.

Risk and Protective Factors

School-aged children are navigating a time of peer pressure and exploration of personal identity. Between the ages of 12 and 18, children are seeking to develop autonomy from parents and gaining personal freedom, while simultaneously seeking to gain approval and social acceptance from their peers and classmates. This time of life can be challenging, and some adolescents may

Table 9.2 Risk Factors for Adolescent Substance Use

Biological factors	• Genetic profile • Family member with an addiction • Personal/family history of mental disorders • Family history of affective disorders and emotional disturbance (e.g., depression or anxiety)
Psychological factors	• Depression or other psychiatric illness • A history of suicide attempts • Low self-esteem • Risk taking behaviors
Social factors	• Parenting style or problems in relationship with parents • Loss of loved ones • Minority status (e.g., gender, race, sexual orientation, or physical/mental disability) • Early sexual experiences • School problems • Problems with peers

Source: Adapted from Doweiko (2002, p. 296) and Sanjuan and Langenbucher (1999, p. 481).

turn to substance use for help in coping with challenges or difficult situations. Others may use for pro-social reasons, and still others may simply experiment with substance use to determine if it is something they would like to incorporate into his or her personal identity. Several risk factors may impact the likelihood of adolescent substances use. Table 9.2 provides examples.

Research About SFBT with Substance Use

The research supporting SFBT as an evidence-based approach continues to grow (Franklin, Trepper, Gingerich, & McCollum, 2012). Several studies now illustrate that SFBT is effective in working with adolescents (Bakhshipour, Aryan, Karami, & Farrokhi, 2011; Franklin, Moore, & Hopson, 2008; King & Reza, 2014), and additional studies demonstrate the effectiveness of SFBT in treating substance use/abuse (Froeschle, Smith, & Ricard, 2007; Smock et al., 2008). One study (Froeschle et al., 2007) specifically illustrated that adolescent females who experienced a 16-week SFBT group showed improvements in drug use, improvements in attitudes toward drugs, and a decrease in home and school behavior issues. SFBT is an effective treatment that meets school-aged children who are using substances where they are and can effectively help to decrease negative effects of such use.

Case Example

Many things make the solution-focused approach different from traditional problem-focused ways of conducting psychotherapy. One of the key differences occurs not only in what the school social worker says to the student but also in how the school social worker listens. While most training materials on this approach focus on the techniques commonly used by solution-focused practitioners, this chapter shifts the focus toward the language used to co-construct a session. Put more simply, knowing about the questions and knowing how to develop them in a conversation with someone who is struggling with a significant issue (in this case, substance use/abuse) are two completely different things. This chapter highlights the later by reviewing a difficult case involving a teenager and his family that involves substance abuse and other defiant behaviors. We include direct portions of the first session in this chapter, summarize what happened in subsequent sessions, and conclude by describing the events that occurred with this teen and his family after therapy was over.

Overview of the SFBT Approach

Before reviewing of the first session, a short overview of the SFBT approach as used by these authors will help readers fully understand what the school social worker is doing in the session and why these activities are helpful to the student. SFBT is very different from traditional problem-focused psychotherapy approaches. The differences are not just in the theory itself but also in what the school social worker is doing in the session with the student, what language the school social worker is specifically using, and what the school social worker is listening for. The language of these sessions is significantly different than the language of traditional counseling sessions. The best way to see this difference is to observe and analyze the sessions being done in this way.

When learning this approach, it is key to study more than the simple techniques (e.g., scaling questions or the miracle question), or the questions commonly asked during counseling. Because SFBT is a co-construction process that develops a description of the student's preferred future, the school social worker will miss the most important part of this way of working—*the language*—if he or she only pays attention to the techniques themselves. The SFBT approach is about developing questions that utilize the student's exact language, utterance by utterance. This may seem obvious and easy, but in practice, it is not.

There is a quote that says, "There is a difference between knowing the path, and walking the path." This is certainly true in using the SFBT approach: knowing about the miracle question does not necessarily equip someone with the ability to develop a miracle question that is unique and useful to the individual student sitting with the school social worker in a session. The most frequently asked question from attendees to lectures is often "How do you ask the miracle to a client who is ...?" This question arises because most people spend a lot of time focusing on learning the techniques and not on language. Yet, the language is what holds the key to mastering this approach, for the language is where this approach happens. SFBT advocates that a school social worker listen and use the student's individual language from each utterance to effectively build individualized questions for each of his or her speaking turns. A better question to ask might be "How do you ask a question if the student says ..."? When we focus on what we say next instead of on what we do next, our learning expands, and we evolve into using this approach beyond just the techniques.

Since the SFBT approach was adequately reviewed earlier, we will not spend too much space here going over the well-known details of this way of working. Instead, we focus on the different facets of a SFBT conversation, what the SFBT school social worker is listening for, and how that information is used in the session. This is done by reviewing the work with a teen who is struggling with substance abuse/misuse issues. It should be noted that the authors of this chapter outline a SFBT session in a fairly structured way. This structure, although different than the one used by many other SFBT clinicians, is consistent with how we work in all SFBT sessions.

The Story of Shawn

Shawn and his family came to counseling after Shawn's recent stay at an inpatient hospital due to several issues that were taking place in his life. Aged 16, Shawn was using marijuana almost daily and occasionally experimented with other, harder drugs. Shawn also had a habit of threatening to kill himself when his parents did not let him do something he really wanted to do, although no actual attempts were reported. These threats were often made for very small, insignificant reasons (e.g., if Shawn wanted to play video games or use marijuana). In short, if Shawn wanted to do it and his parents said no, he would explode. Even though these explosions would occur over just about anything, nothing set him off more consistently or significantly than when his parents did not let him hang out with his friends. These incidents would include yelling, loads of screaming, and on occasion, some pushing and grabbing between Shawn and his father. This was the case in the incident that sent Shawn to the hospital and led his family to counseling.

When the family arrived for the first session, it was immediately clear that Shawn did not want to be there, and his parents looked as if they were at their wits' end. The parents entered the room first and informed me (E.C.) of all of the things they have been dealing with. Shawn informed his parents that he would not talk to me with the parents present, so the family asked if I would be willing to see the teen alone. I agreed. What follows is a review of that conversation.

Stage 1: Establish the Desired Outcome from the Talk

As Shawn walked in to the room, he clearly was not very pleased to be in my office. The first task of the SFBT counselor is the same, however, despite the level of motivation of the client: ask questions to identify what the teen's desired outcome is from the session. Attending to this task focuses the conversation on the future and the changes the student would like to see, rather than focusing on the problem that led the student to come to counseling.

> **Elliott:** Can I call you Shawn? Is that okay?
>
> **Shawn:** Yeah, that's fine.
>
> **Elliott:** So, what are your best hopes from our talking?
>
> **Shawn:** Umm, I don't know.
>
> **Elliott:** Umm.
>
> **Shawn:** I mean to be honest, I really don't want to be here.
>
> **Elliott:** Well, since you are here and we will be talking for a bit, what is your best hope from our talk?
>
> **Shawn:** What do you mean?
>
> **Elliott:** Well, if you and I were to have a helpful conversation, what difference would you like it to make in your life?
>
> **Shawn:** As in what way?
>
> **Elliott:** Not sure. I suppose that would be up to you.
>
> **Shawn:** Umm, I don't know
>
> **Elliott:** What do you think?
>
> **Shawn:** But what will we be talking about?

Elliott: Not sure yet. I guess whatever differences you'd be pleased to see in your life.

Shawn: Okay. I guess anything helps.

Elliott: Umm, and if it does help, what differences would you like it to make for you?

Shawn: Umm, I guess I could be more positive.

Elliott: Okay, so how would you notice yourself becoming more positive?

Shawn: I don't know, but I think it would be a good thing.

Elliott: A good thing. Well, how would you know it was a good thing? What would you notice taking place that would tell you that this good thing is happening?

Shawn: Just a positive change, I guess.

Elliott: What positive change?

Shawn: Umm, I don't know.

Elliott: What do you think Shawn?

Shawn: Umm, I don't know. It all depends on what we are talking about, I guess.

Elliott: That makes sense. I am not quite sure yet, either, but you did say becoming more positive would be a good thing, right?

Shawn: Yes.

Elliott: So, how would you notice you are, in fact, becoming more positive?

Shawn: Umm, not using drugs.

Elliott: What would you be doing instead of drugs?

Shawn: Umm, I'm not sure. Maybe spending more time working on my school work.

Elliott: Really?

Shawn: Yeah.

Elliott: And if you found yourself, somehow, not quite sure how yet, but somehow, after our talk involved in more school work and less drugs, would you consider that more positive?

Shawn: Yeah.

Elliott: Umm, what would the impact be of you spending more time working on schoolwork?

Shawn: I'm pretty sure my grades would be higher.

Elliott: Okay, how high might they be able to get?

Shawn: I don't know. Very high I think. [laughs]

Elliott: [laughs] How long has it been since you worked on your schoolwork in this way?

Shawn: A long time.

Elliott: But you've done it before?

Shawn: Yeah.

Elliott: So, if you find yourself spending more time doing this, that would be a good change for you?

Shawn: Yeah, it would be.

Elliott: What other changes would you notice that would be in line with being more positive?

Shawn: Umm, more freedom.

Elliott: Umm, and where would this freedom come from?

Shawn: My parents.

Elliott: Are they the only ones that would be pleased to see you more positive?

Shawn: At the moment, yeah.

Elliott: Okay, okay, and what would you do with the freedom that would come along with being more positive?

Shawn: Umm, hang out with friends and that sort of stuff.

Elliott: Okay, so if somehow our chatting lead to you being more positive and hanging out more with your friends, you would look back and be pleased that we have met?

Shawn: Yeah.

Elliott: You would look back and be pleased that we had this chat?

Shawn: Yeah.

Elliott: And how would you know that your parents had noticed you being more positive?

Shawn: I don't know. They would probably be more happy, I suppose.

Elliott: How would you notice they were happy?

Shawn: They would be smiling.

Elliott: And how would you respond to their smiling?

Shawn: I would smile as well.

Elliott: And what do you imagine each of you smiling more would do to your household?

Shawn: It makes us all so much more happy.

Elliott: So, if our talking not only lead to being more positive and spending more time with friends and you being more focused on schoolwork instead of using drugs, if it also caused you to be happier and caused happiness to come out of your parents, would you be pleased that we had chatted?

Shawn: Yes, for sure.

As you can see from this segment of the session, I was able to ask questions that shifted the focus of the conversation away from the student's frustration and toward Shawn's desired outcome for the session. Although it was originally difficult at first to get Shawn to express what he was hoping to get out of the session, I persisted in doing two important things: 1) trusting the student's ability to answer the questions about what his best hopes were, and 2) using the student's exact language to continually move the session away from problem-talk and toward an identification of his best hopes. Although a student may be using drugs, the SFBT counselor will not overtly ask about this issue (unless the student mentions it, like Shawn does) but, rather, will trust that having a solution-building conversation about the student's preferred future will help that student make changes leading to the fulfillment of this preferred future. For school-aged youth, this process can help reduce anxiety and/or "resistance," and it can help them to know the SFBT counselor is interested in their uniqueness and desires rather than pushing a preconceived plan for what will be useful and helpful. This approach also individualizes the treatment for each unique student.

Stage 2: Picking Up the Client Language

After the desired outcome has been identified, the next task in the process is for the school social worker to educate him- or herself about the student's language. Notice that I did not say anything about the student's problem, or even their strengths during the first portion of the session. The SFBT counselor is interested in the specific language the student uses as well as the names of key people in the student's life. This attention to and use of the student's language helps the school social worker be a more informed professional and more able to develop helpful questions for each individual student as the session unfolds.

Solution-Focused Brief Therapy in Schools

The session continues:

Elliott: Awesome. Well, before we chat about that stuff, can I get to know you a little bit, is that okay?

Shawn: Yeah.

Elliott: What is your best friend's name, Shawn?

Shawn: Mike.

Elliott: Mike? Wonderful. And umm, what do you do for fun?

Shawn: Umm, I'm not sure. I'm not allowed to do much at the moment.

Elliott: Not allowed?

Shawn: Yeah, I've been punished for a while.

Elliott: Oh, wow.

Shawn: That's why I mentioned wanting freedom.

Elliott: Oh, I see.

Shawn: I'd like to get back doing stuff with Mike and hanging out, but my parents never let me do anything.

Elliott: Okay, that makes since.

Shawn: Yeah, they overreact a lot.

Elliott: [laughs] Perhaps. What is the best thing I should know about you and Mike?

Shawn: Umm, he keeps me positive.

Elliott: How does he do that?

Shawn: I don't know. We've just been friends a long time, and he can calm me down.

Elliott: Has he always had this ability with you?

Shawn: Yeah, as long as I've known him anyway.

Elliott: Very nice. And you mentioned doing more school work, what is your favorite class?

Shawn: Umm, History.

Elliott: What is it about that one?

Shawn: I don't know. I just like it. Sort of always fascinated me.

Elliott: What is your favorite thing about history?

Shawn: Hmm, not sure. I just like learning about different people and places.

Elliott: Have you ever thought about what you would like to be do for a living when you get older?

Shawn: Nah, not really.

Elliott: If you take a moment to think about it now, what comes to mind?

Shawn: Who knows, college, maybe, I guess.

Elliott: Really? What makes you say that?

Shawn: I guess if things worked out I'd like to go and would probably like it. I just haven't thought about it much until you just asked me.

Elliott: How often do you focus on schoolwork these days?

Shawn: Umm, lately, not too much to be honest.

Elliott: Okay, and at your best, how much time might you spending?

Shawn: Not sure. More time than I spending now for sure, at least some time per day.

Elliott: Would you be pleased to be doing this?

Shawn: No, no, umm, it would be boring, but it would feel good I think to be doing something productive.

Elliott: And what type of skills do you possess that would allow you to be able to do this?

Shawn: I used to do this all of the time, so I know I can do it. Plus, I'm smart enough. I just haven't tried.

Elliott: So you know you have it in you.

Shawn: Yeah, so I just have to make some changes.

Elliott: Okay, I see.

Shawn: Yeah.

Elliott: Umm, so what would you say is your best quality? For somebody who is just getting to know you, like I am today, what is the very best thing about you, the thing you're proudest of or pleased with?

Shawn: I'm different.

Elliott: How so?

Shawn: I'm just different. I don't know. I'm just different from a lot of people at my school.

Elliott: Do you like being different?

Shawn: Umm, I don't want to be like everybody else, just an everyday person. I wanna be different.

Elliott: Have you always been like that?

Shawn: Yeah, always.

Elliott: And you're pleased about that?

Shawn: Yeah.

Elliott: And what do you know about yourself that lets you know that one day you can live without drugs in your life?

Shawn: Because I could do it before, so I can do it.

Elliott: How did you do it before?

Shawn: Umm, I think the social scene I was in. I got myself out of the social scene. I'm just trying to find friends who are not into that sort of stuff, are more positive and make me do stuff. Do you know what I mean?

Elliott: Yes.

Shawn: I think it is more about, having people behind you that push you to doing the positive things instead of doing the drugs.

Elliott: And has it worked for you? Have you gotten away from that social group?

Shawn: Yeah, mostly.

Elliott: That has worked well for you. How did you do that? How did you know how to do that?

Shawn: I've been talking to my school counselor about the whole thing, too, but I suppose it is just, umm, you just know in yourself that it is the wrong thing to do, the wrong type of people. And the more you associate yourself with those types of people, then you are going to keep using, and it's going to repeat itself.

Elliott: And you don't want to be like everyone else, right?

Shawn: Right. I started drugs a while ago. and it just got more and more.

Elliott: Yeah. and somehow you knew it was wrong?

Shawn: Yeah, plus I started behaving in a way that wasn't like me. Skipping school, failing classes, things like that.

Elliott: Was Mike coming along with you?

Shawn: No, he got mad at me, and we lost touch for a while.

Elliott: Did that bother you?

Shawn: Yeah.

Elliott: Does he know how important he is to you?

Shawn: I don't think so. I think he's still upset with me, but we text sometimes.

Elliott: Would he be pleased to see you being more positive and doing your schoolwork and things like that?

Shawn: Yeah.

Elliott: How would he let you know he was pleased?

Shawn: Umm, he'd probably talk to me more and want to hang out and stuff.

Elliott: Would you be pleased if you talked more and hung out again?

Shawn: Yes, very!

Notice that in this part of the session how I learned a lot of information that increased my skill in asking questions of Shawn, including specific things I needed to ask Shawn that would be inappropriate to ask anyone else about. For example, I was able to uncover names of key people in the student's life (Mike), information about what the student enjoys (hanging out and history), as well as what the student likes most about himself (being different). I also now know what the student believes about drug use (that having people behind you will help) as well as what thoughts he has about his current use (Mike does not like it; drug use has changed his behavior).

These details may seem like insignificant information, but in this approach, this sort of information is key. It helps the school social worker develop more tailored, specific questions that are just for one unique client. In turn, this allows the conversation to feel less like an onslaught of techniques and much more like a helpful and therapeutic, co-constructed conversation.

Stage 3: The Preferred Future Description

Even if you are only minimally familiar with the solution-focused approach, you have probably heard of the miracle question. This is the part of the session when the student is asked a future-focused question to elicit a detailed description of his or her preferred future. This is the most important part of the SFBT session. In the session with Shawn, which continues here, notice that the question is asked using information that was learned in the previous stages and that it involves the presence of the student's best hopes.

Elliott: Can I ask you an unusual question? So, umm, suppose tonight, as you sleep, a miracle happens that somehow kind of changes your life in all positive ways and makes you the very best version of Shawn that you want to be, the type of guy who is being more positive, doing his school work, earning more freedoms, and being just the kind a guy you want to be. But this miracle happened as you slept, right? So you couldn't know it happened.

Elliott: So, when you woke up the next day, what would be the first thing you noticed that would tell you "I am in this different world where I am the very, very, very best version of myself and moving in a different, much more positive direction"?

Shawn: I wouldn't think of drugs when I woke up.

Elliott: Would you think of instead?

Shawn: I don't know.

Elliott: What do you think?

Shawn: Umm, it's a hard question. I don't really know.

Elliott: Yeah, it's hard, an odd question even. But what do you think? You would wake up and wouldn't be thinking of drugs, so what would you be thinking of instead?

Shawn: School, maybe.

Elliott: School? What about school would you be thinking about?

Shawn: I don't know. What I had to do on that day, I think.

Elliott: What types of things would you have to do for school on this day?

Shawn: Not really sure. I have a lot of work to do.

Elliott: Really?

Shawn: Yeah, it's been a while since I've thought about this stuff.

Elliott: What is the first thing you would do?

Shawn: Get up, I guess?

Elliott: And how would you know you were getting up as the very best version of you?

Shawn: I don't know. I'd have energy, maybe.

Elliott: What time would you be waking up?

Shawn: Hmmm, around 7 AM I think.

Elliott: And after waking up at 7 AM as the very best version of yourself?

Shawn: The fact that I would be awake at all at this time would be the first sign.

Elliott: So, it would be unusual for you on this day to wake up at this time, and instead of thinking about drugs, to be thinking about school and what you have to do?

Shawn: Yes, very.

Elliott: And what is the first thing you would do?

Shawn: I'd get dressed, I think.

Elliott: And what would be different about the way you got dressed when you were at your very best and had energy?

Shawn: I would turn on the radio as I got dressed.

Elliott: What would you listen to?

Shawn: Not sure. Whatever I was in the mood for.

Elliott: What might you be in the mood for do you think?

Shawn: Rap. Maybe Lil Wayne or Drake.

Elliott: What one might you be leaning toward?

Shawn: Drake.

Elliott: What else would you notice about yourself as you were getting dressed listening to Drake?

Shawn: I would be smiling and singing along as I was getting dressed, maybe even loudly.

Elliott: Would you be pleased by this?

Shawn: Yeah, I think so.

Elliott: You'd be loud. Would anyone hear?

Shawn: [laughing] Yeah, my mom.

Elliott: Would she find this to be a big surprise or a little surprise?

Shawn: Big, definitely big.

Elliott: And how would she respond?

Shawn: I don't know. I think she'd think I was on something.

Elliott: How would you notice that in fact you are not on anything, you are just back to being your very best?

Shawn: It would be on my face.

Elliott: In what way, what would be different about your face?

Shawn: I would be smiling for real. You know, like the type of smile that let's people know you're for real happy.

Elliott: Would she be pleased to see this?

Shawn: I don't know. I mean. I think so. She hasn't seen me like that in a while, but I think she would be very happy.

Elliott: How would she let you know she was happy?

Shawn: She'd smile back at me. She might ask me to turn the music down or stop singing, but she would be smiling as she said it. Not mad, you know?

Elliott: Yeah. How would you respond to that?

Shawn: I would do what she asked, but not with an attitude. I would just do it.

Elliott: And would that surprise her?

Shawn: For me not to have an attitude? Yeah, she would be very surprised. It would change the whole morning.

Elliott: In what way?

Shawn: Well, we wouldn't be fighting. There'd be no yelling. It just wouldn't be so negative around the house.

Elliott: Would anyone else notice?

Shawn: It's just me, my mother, and my father in the house, so I'm sure my father would notice.

Elliott: How would he notice?

Shawn: He would notice we weren't fighting.

Elliott: What would you and your mom are doing on this morning?

Shawn: Just getting along, being nice to each other.

Elliott: How would he let you know he was pleased?

Shawn: He would definitely say something.

Elliott: Like what?

Shawn: He would come in and talk with us. He would say how happy he was we weren't fighting. He's like that, he says stuff like that.

Elliott: Would you be pleased with this interaction with him?

Shawn: Yeah.

Elliott: How would you let him know you were pleased?

Shawn: Honestly, I would ask him if he wanted to have breakfast with me. We used to do that sort of thing.

Elliott: What would you two have for breakfast on this day?

Shawn: Toast or something.

Elliott: As you had this breakfast, what would be different about the way you interacted?

Shawn: We'd be talking. You know, talking like friends. Liking each other.

Elliott: Would you be pleased by this?

Shawn: Yeah.

Elliott: How would you let your father know you were pleased?

Shawn: I would tell him how nice it was to be interacting the way we used to.

Elliott: How would he respond to this?

Shawn: He'd probably cry, you know. I might, too.

Elliott: How long would this meal last?

Shawn: Ten or 15 minutes or so. I have to get to school, and he has to get to work.

Elliott: How do you get to school?

Shawn: My mom.

Elliott: Before you know, how would your mom and dad know that Shawn-at-his-best was heading to school?

Shawn: I'd grab my books, and during breakfast, I would have been talking about all I planned to accomplish in the day.

Elliott: Really? How much of a change would that be?

Shawn: Huge.

Elliott: And as you and your mom head toward the school, how would she notice that the changes she saw in the morning were still a part of you?

Shawn: We'd be talking in the car about my schoolwork. I wouldn't be mad or frustrated by her questions. I would just answer them.

Elliott: How long is the drive to school?

Shawn: Not too long. We live close to school. They just drive me because they don't trust me to go all of the time.

Elliott: Okay, and when you got to the school, who would be the first person to notice something was different about you?

Shawn: Mike.

Elliott: How would he notice?

Solution-Focused Brief Therapy in Schools

Shawn: Because I would not hang around the bad kids and I would walk right up to him, before the first class.

Elliott: How would he know that he was talking to the very best version of Shawn?

Shawn: He would just know.

Elliott: But how?

Shawn: I don't know.

Elliott: What do you think?

Shawn: I think I would apologize honestly. I think I would even ask him to be friends again.

Elliott: How would he respond?

Shawn: I think he'd like it.

Elliott: Really?

Shawn: I'd have to promise him I would stay away from the bad kids and not use drugs.

Elliott: Would you?

Shawn: Yeah, if I were my very best, I wouldn't even want to do those things.

Elliott: Cool. What would happen next?

Shawn: Mike and I would walk to class together like we used to.

Elliott: You guys are in the same class?

Shawn: Yeah, we have the same homeroom class, the first one of the day.

Elliott: When you got to class, how would the teacher notice that you were different? That you were the best version of yourself.

Shawn: I would sit next to Mike. He sits in the front of the class and pays attention to what she says. He really is a good student, a good kid really.

Elliott: Would she be pleased to see you sitting in the front of the class?

Shawn: Yeah. She would say "Welcome!" or something like that.

Elliott: What would be different about the way you conducted yourself while sitting in the front of the class?

Shawn: I would be focused and paying attention instead of on my phone or goofing around.

Elliott: What difference would that make for you?

Shawn: Huge. It would feel good to be acting the way I used to.

Elliott: Would other teachers notice?

Shawn: Yeah, all of them would.

Elliott: Would any of the others say anything?

Shawn: Maybe. I would just have to see. I know my history teacher would for sure, though.

Elliott: How would your history teacher notice?

Shawn: I'd be enthusiastic about it again. I really do like that class.

Elliott: Yeah. It is your favorite right?

Shawn: Yeah.

Elliott: So how would you show the history teacher that your enthusiasm was back?

Shawn: I would be interacting, asking questions and raising my hand. You know, that sort of stuff.

Elliott: What else?

Shawn: You know, just back being involved.

Elliott: So what would be different about when the school day ended?

Shawn: I'd find Mike again for sure.

Elliott: Really? Then what?

Shawn: I'd see if he wanted to hang out after school.

Elliott: What would you suggest the two of you do?

Shawn: Honestly?

Elliott: Yeah. What would you like to do with him?

Shawn: I'd ask him if he wanted to come over and do our homework together and then maybe play video games.

Elliott: Would he be surprised to hear you suggest this?

Shawn: Yeah.

Elliott: How would you guys get back to your house?

Shawn: We'd walk. He lives in my neighborhood, too.

Elliott: What would be different about the way the two of you walked home? Like, what would you be talking about?

Shawn: To be honest, it wouldn't feel different at all. We used to do this everyday, and it would just feel normal to be doing it again. We would be talking about new video games and stuff like that.

Solution-Focused Brief Therapy in Schools

Elliott: Would this be another version of the positive changes you mentioned earlier?

Shawn: Yeah, definitely.

Elliott: When you reached your house, would anyone be home?

Shawn: No, not for the first 30 minute or so. We would be there alone when my mother got home from work.

Elliott: And when she got home, what would she find that would look to her like evidence that her son was still at his very best?

Shawn: Me and Mike would be sitting at the dining room table doing our homework.

Elliott: And would this be a big surprise or a little surprise to her?

Shawn: Huge!

Elliott: Would she be pleased by this huge surprise?

Shawn: Yes, definitely.

Elliott: How would she let you know that she was pleased?

Shawn: She would be very nice to Mike. My parents love him. She would offer us something to eat, I think.

Elliott: Really? Like what?

Shawn: A snack or something. She may even ask him to stay for dinner.

Elliott: Okay, is that a good thing, do you think?

Shawn: Yeah, man, we used to do this all the time. Wow.

Elliott: How long do you think it would take you guys to finish your homework?

Shawn: Umm, maybe an hour or so.

Elliott: Really?

Shawn: Yeah.

Elliott: Then what would you guys do?

Shawn: I'd ask my mom if I could play video games with Mike while she was cooking dinner.

Elliott: What do your think she'd say?

Shawn: I am not too sure. I think she'd say yes to be honest.

Elliott: Really?

Shawn: Yeah. I mean, I've been grounded for a while, but if all of this happened, I really think she would let me and Mike play the game. Plus, I think she would be happy that he is back around.

Elliott: Okay, that makes sense. What would you and Mike play?

Shawn: Madden, definitely.

Elliott: PlayStation or Xbox.

Shawn: I like the PlayStation. He has an Xbox.

Elliott: Who would win?

Shawn: [laughing] Me, for sure.

Elliott: What difference would it make for you to be back playing video games with Mike in the way that you guys always have?

Shawn: It would make a big difference. Even as I sit here, it seems so normal. Like something I should be doing all of the time.

Elliott: So, that would be a good thing?

Shawn: Yeah, for sure.

Elliott: What might your mother make for dinner on that day?

Shawn: She makes a lot of things. My favorite is spaghetti.

Elliott: What would be different about dinner on this day?

Shawn: To be honest, nothing. This is all just so normal, just like the way things used to be. My dad would come home right about the time dinner was ready, and we would all eat together.

Elliott: And how would your father notice that things were back the way they used to be?

Shawn: It would be obvious, I think. Mike would be there, my mom would tell him I had already done my homework. You know, just normal.

Elliott: What else would you discuss during the dinner?

Shawn: Nothing really. We would talk about sports, TV. You know, fun stuff.

Elliott: Would you enjoy this?

Shawn: Yeah, I'd love it.

Elliott: How would you show this to Mike and your parents?

Shawn: I'd be smiling the whole time.

Elliott: I see. What would happen after dinner?

Shawn: Well, Mike would have to head home. I'd walk him to the door and plan on meeting him in the morning. Either we'd walk to school together, or if my parents don't let me walk he would ride with me.

Elliott: Okay, I see. Then what would happen?

Shawn: Well, it would be getting pretty late, I think, so I would help my parents clean the kitchen and start getting ready for bed.

Elliott: How different would this be?

Shawn: It would be huge because we always fight and there is always a lot of yelling at night. This night would just be peaceful and quiet. Just a good way to end the day.

Elliott: I see. What would be different about the end of your day and the way you got ready for bed?

Shawn: I would just have peace and be relaxed. It would be nice to be so calm.

Elliott: Well, thank you, Shawn, for answering all of my questions. Do you mind if I take a minute to write my thoughts down?

Shawn: No, that's fine.

Notice how at this point of the session, the emphasis is on the description related to the detailed presence of the student's preferred future, not how the student can make the changes that lead toward this becoming a reality. It is simply about the description. This is one of the major distinctions between solution building and problem solving. SFBT is not an approach that involves problem solving. By engaging in a solution-building conversation, the client is more likely to experience, in the moment, the thoughts, feelings, and emotions that he or she will likely re-experience when the best hopes occur. In this conversation, the school social worker will experience with the student a change in how the mood of the conversation shifts. The school social worker will also notice how the student begins to express that the changes seem "like normal." This comes about due to the great details elicited while answering the questions and makes it more likely the student will make changes that lead toward the desired future.

Also notice that the focus is not using drugs and that this is hardly mentioned during this conversation. In a SFBT session, the focus should remain on what will be present rather than on what will not. By focusing on what Shawn will be doing on a day when his best hopes occur, we avoid all problem-talk—even if that problem-talk is the reason for the referral. Instead of this problem-talk, we have an enjoyable conversation about Shawn at his best. This is a conversation that Shawn is interested in having, thus eliminating the need to worry about what to do with a "resistant" client.

Stage 4: Session Wrap Up

The key to this part of the session is to provide feedback in line with the information that has been discussed. It is important to provide feedback that allows the student to remain the "expert" of the session, that is significant to the student, and that is in the student's own words. During this part of the session, the school social worker also may offer a task to the student. In this approach, however, it is important to make a suggestion that is simple and usually just about noticing the discussed changes. This kind of suggestion does not remove the student's autonomy.

The session concludes:

> **Elliott:** Sorry to keep you waiting.
> **Shawn:** That's alright.
> **Elliott:** Umm, Shawn, first I want to say what a pleasure it was to talk with you. I know you did not want to be here at first, but I appreciate that were patient with me and answered all of my questions.
> **Shawn:** I enjoyed it, actually.
> **Elliott:** Great, I'm glad to hear that. You know, there were a few things about you that stood out to me. The first is that you seem to be so much more than the troubles that have been bothering you. It seems to me that you like being at your best much more than having the problems that have plagued you recently. The more you talked about your parents being happy and spending time with Mike, the more it felt like that is the real you. Sort of like who you really are and who you'd like to be.
> **Shawn:** Yeah, I've just been so stupid lately.
> **Elliott:** Well, how do you feel about noticing some of the changes we discussed today and when they actually happen, and see what difference that would make for you?
> **Shawn:** I'd like that.

Elliott: Excellent. Would you mind if I talked to your parents for a second?

Shawn: Not at all.

Elliott: It was a pleasure to meet you.

Shawn: Likewise.

At the end of the session, I had a brief chat with the parents and informed them that Shawn's mood seemed to shift during the session, and that he was more interested in making changes in his life. I asked the family to notice his changes and praise him for them.

The family attended one more session two weeks later and could not believe the changes Shawn had made in his life. He had been hanging around with Mike and doing his homework daily. His grades and mood had drastically improved as well. To the family's surprise, they did not think they needed another session.

It is important to remember when working with youth who are using substances that we cannot be scared or intimidated by their presenting problem. Instead, we need to remember that if we have a meaningful conversation about what the student's best hopes are and what he or she will notice when those best hopes happen, we are being solution focused. We need to remember that this kind of conversation allows us to speak to the real kid, not just a kid using drugs.

Resources

Bakhshipour, B., Aryan, S.K., Karami, A., & Farrokhi, N. (2011). The effectiveness of solution-focused therapy on reducing behavioral problems of the elementary and brief therapy and high school students at Sari. *Counseling Research and Development, 10*(37), 7–24.

Doweiko, H. E. (2002). *Concepts of chemical dependency* (5th ed.). Pacific Grove, CA: Brooks/Cole.

Franklin, C., Moore, K., & Hopson, L. (2008). Effectiveness of solution-focused brief therapy in a school setting. *Children and Schools, 30*(1), 15–26.

Franklin, C., Trepper, T. S., Gingerich, W. J., & McCollum, E. E. (2012). *Solution-focused brief therapy: A handbook of evidence-based practice.* New York, NY: Oxford University Press.

Froeschle, J. G., Smith, R. L., & Ricard, R. (2007). The efficacy of a systematic substance abuse program for adolescent females. *Professional School Counseling, 10*, 498–505.

King, Z., & Reza, A. (2014). The effectiveness of training solution-focused approach to increasing the level of social adjustment of adolescent identity crisis. *Journal of Women and Society, 17*(5), 21–40.

Office of Applied Studies. (2013). *Results from the 2008 National Survey on Drug Use and Health*. Rockville, MD: Substance Abuse and Mental Health Services Administration.

Sanjuan, P. M., & Langenbucher, J. W. (1999). Age-limited populations: Youth, adolescents, and older adults. In B. S. McCrady & E. E. Epstein (Eds.). *Addiction: A comprehensive guidebook* (pp. 477–498). New York, NY: Oxford University Press.

Smock, S. A., Trepper, T. S., Wetchler, J. L., McCollum, E. E., Ray, R., & Pierce, K. (2008). Solution-focused group therapy for level 1 substance abusers. *Journal of Marital and Family Therapy, 34*(1), 107–120.

US Department of Health and Human Services. (2008). *Treatment of adolescents with substance use disorders*. Substance Abuse and Mental Health Services Administration, Center for Substance Abuse Treatment: Rockville, MD.

10

■ ■ ■

SFBT in Action
Eating Disorders

Karrie Slavin & Johnny S. Kim

Definitions and Descriptions

Eating disorders are not very widespread among the general population (Smink, van Hoeken, & Hoek, 2012) but have been identified as one of the most frequent issues encountered by school social workers (Kelly et al., 2015). Eating disorders are mostly associated with mental health problems that can negatively affect a student's physical, emotional, and mental health (Stice, Marti, & Durant, 2011). While eating disorders are mostly prevalent in Caucasian females, increases in eating disorders have been reported among African Americans, Latinos, and Asian Americans (Alegria et al., 2007; Heller & Lu, 2015; Shuttlesworth & Zotter, 2009). Additionally, males now account for anywhere between 10% and 25% of all cases, with male athletes at higher risk (Heller & Lu, 2015). The three most central types of eating disorders are anorexia nervosa (AN), bulimia nervosa (BN), and binge-eating disorder (BED).

Prevalence rates for AN are estimated at 0.4% among young females (American Psychological Association, 2013). The *Diagnostic and Statistical Manual of Mental Disorders, Fifth edition* (DSM-5) defines AN using the following three criteria: 1) significantly low body weight due to restriction of energy intake given age, gender, and physical health; 2) intense fear of gaining weight, or persistent behaviors to hinder weight gain; and 3) disturbance in the way one perceives the self's body weight or shape, undue influence of body weight or shape on self-evaluation, or absence of recognition of the seriousness of current low body weight. In essence, a student maintains an unhealthy body weight that is below the normal level for age, gender, and physical health. Within AN are two subtypes called restricting type and binge-eating/purging type. Restricting type involves weight loss through dieting, fasting, and/or excessive exercise. Binge-eating/purging type involves binge-eating or purging behavior, such as self-induced vomiting, misuse of laxatives, diuretics, or enemas (APA, 2013).

The second common eating disorder school social workers frequently encounter is BN. Prevalence rates for BN are slightly higher than those for AN and are estimated at 1% to 1.5% among young females (APA, 2013). BN involves three essential features:

1. Recurrent episodes of binge eating (i.e., eating large amounts of food in a short period of time, lack of control on amount or type of food consumed).
2. Reoccurring inappropriate behaviors to prevent weight gain (i.e., purging behaviors).
3. Self-evaluation overly influenced by body shape and weight.

To meet the DSM-5 criteria for BN, the binge-eating and purging behaviors need to occur an average of once per week for three months (APA, 2013). Unlike AN, students suffering from BN are typically of normal weight to overweight for their age and gender (Frank, 2015).

The third type of eating disorder school social workers are likely to encounter is BED. The prevalence rates for BED among adult (18 years and older) females are estimated at 1.6%, with rates of 0.8% among adult males (APA, 2013). According to the DSM-5, BED must occur at least once a week for three months, and the student must experience marked distress regarding binge eating. Additionally, there must be recurrent episodes of binge eating, as described earlier for BN. The key distinguishing criteria for BED is that binge-eating episodes are associated with three or more of the following:

- Rapid eating beyond normal for the student.
- Eating until feeling uncomfortably full.
- Eating large quantities of food when not hungry.
- Eating by oneself due to embarrassment over the large amount of food being consumed.
- Feeling disgusted with oneself, depressed, or guilty after binge eating.

All these criteria need to be met in order have the diagnosis of BED (APA, 2013).

What Causes Eating Disorders

Eating disorders typically occur during adolescence and young adulthood and can continue into adulthood (Frank, 2015). Currently, we have little understanding about the exact cause of eating disorders, but many ideas have been posited to help understand this problem. Recent research shows that some students may be more genetically predisposed to eating disorders than others (Pomeroy & Browning, 2013). An article by Frank (2015) reviewed two recent studies on AN and BM using magnetic resonance imaging to compare brain images from girls and women diagnosed with one of the two eating disorders with brain images from a group of healthy girls and women. Frank reports, "The studies highlight that acute AN and BN are associated with widespread alterations in cortical structure across the brain, primarily reductions in cortical volume or thickness, but the BN sample also showed areas of larger volume, raising the question whether this condition is associated with white matter reorganization or altered development" (p. 602). The understanding of eating disorders from a genetic and physiological perspective is still in its infancy, however, and limited due to inconsistent definitions of diagnoses and symptoms, but it continues to gain much attention as science advances (Trace, Baker, Penas-Lledo, & Bulik, 2013).

Most research has focused on examining psychosocial factors, which has provided a more robust understanding of eating disorders. Several research studies have pointed to concerns around body image and pressures to follow an ideal of thinness (Frank, 2015) as a cause. Students exposed to an ideal body image that is thin often internalize this ideal, and the resulting weight concerns contribute to developing an eating disorder (Keel & Forney, 2013). A research article by Stice, Marti, and Durant (2011) further elaborates:

> This model posits that perceived pressure to be thin from family, peers, and the media and internalization of the thin beauty ideal produce body dissatisfaction. This body dissatisfaction theoretically promotes unhealthy dieting behaviors that may progress to anorexia nervosa. Further, individuals may think dietary restrictions for circumscribed periods permits them to binge eat but not gain weight, which might promote a cycle of acute restriction punctuated by overeating." (p. 623)

Besides body image influences, other risk factors also have been identified and are useful for understanding eating disorders. Weight concern is considered to be a common and consistent risk factor for eating disorders (Keel & Forney, 2013). For example, adolescent girls in the upper 24% of body dissatisfaction group were four times more likely to develop an eating disorder (Stice et al., 2011). Additionally, 11.2% of college-aged woman who reported high levels of weight concern developed an eating disorder within three years (Jacobi et al., 2011).

Peer groups are another important risk factor for eating disorders among students. It is common for students to socialize and interact with other students who share similar interests and values. This peer socialization has the potential to reinforce or exacerbate concerns about body weight and shape among girls and boys, creating a climate that influences behaviors that can lead to students developing eating disorders (Keel & Forney, 2013). For example, a longitudinal study by Zalta and Keel (2006) examined the effects of peer selection and socialization on bulimic symptoms in college students and found that personality factors played a significant role in peer selection, which then led to those selected peers influencing bulimic symptoms.

Reasons for Using the SFBT Approach

There are many ways to help students suffering from eating disorders, and treatment interventions come from the medical, mental health, public health, and social work perspectives. Pomeroy and Browning (2013) note the different types of interventions used to address eating disorders, such as pharmacological interventions, psychoeducational programs, experiential therapies (e.g., art and movement therapy), nutritional therapy, family therapy, cognitive-behavioral therapy, dialectical behavioral therapy, and training in social problem-solving skills. The ultimate goal for many of these interventions is to restore a healthy body image by correcting distorted thinking and providing psychoeducation to help clients change behaviors that will lead to healthy physical functioning (Pomeroy & Browning, 2013).

SFBT provides an alternative way to engage students with eating disorders and can be used as the sole treatment modality or in conjunction with other treatments (e.g., psychoeducation, family therapy, or nutritional therapy). Rather than dwelling on students' negative thoughts or beliefs, SFBT focuses on helping students identify what they want (their preferred future) when the problem is no longer there and how they've made that happen in the past (exceptions). This can be especially useful for students with eating disorders because, when traditional therapy modalities are used, it is reported that many students try to conceal or deny their problems and avoid seeking counseling help (Smink et al., 2012). Because of its collaborative nature and its emphasis on the client's worldview, goal definitions, and resources, SFBT enhances cooperation during the change process (Martin, Guterman, & Shantz, 2012). It engages students in a non-defensive manner and allows students to detail what they want their goals to be and the concrete steps to make their goals happen.

Case Example

The following is a case example of a school social worker utilizing SFBT in a first session with a student experiencing an eating disorder.

Background Information

Jessica is a 16-year-old junior at Central Valley High School. A straight-A student, she competes on the varsity cross-country team and the varsity swim team, and she designs sets for Central Valley's drama club. She has always done well in school and has seemed happy and well adjusted, so this is her first time speaking with the school social worker.

Section 1: Starting the Conversation

> **School Social Worker (SSW):** Hi, Jessica, it's nice to see you today. Thanks for coming in.
>
> **Jessica:** You're welcome. Thanks for seeing me.
>
> **SSW:** You're welcome! So, it looks like from your file that your grades are excellent—good for you. And you made varsity this year for swimming, wow.
>
> **Jessica:** [shyly] Yeah, and for cross country.
>
> **SSW:** Oh, my gosh, how did you get to be such a good athlete?
>
> **Jessica:** Well, lots of practice, I guess, and it's in my genes. My mom was a tennis champ in high school, and my dad was on the football team.

In Section 1, the school social worker focuses on starting the conversation in a way that connects with the student and immediately conveys caring and respect. She does this by thanking the student for coming in and by asking about her strengths. By starting the conversation this way, the school social worker is showing that she sees the student as a whole person and wants to know things about her before finding out about the student's problem. She also has the opportunity to compliment the student, which is an important SFBT technique that functions to "draw clients' attention to their strengths and past successes that might be useful in achieving their goals" (p. 35), while also helping them to "grow more hopeful and confident" (De Jong & Berg, 2008, p. 35).

Section 2: Beginning to Define what the Student Wants to Have Different

> **SSW:** Oh, so genes and practice, huh? That's great. So then, before we go any further, let me just ask you, in terms of your visit today, how are you hoping that I can be helpful to you?
>
> **Jessica:** Umm, well, I really came in because my friend Tia wanted me to. She had um, noticed that I, well—it's dumb, I feel dumb even saying it. I can't say it.
>
> **SSW:** Hey, that's okay. I think it's really cool that you were brave enough to decide to even come in here today. How did you get yourself to do that?
>
> **Jessica:** Well, I guess I knew that Tia is right. I need some help.
>
> **SSW:** Okay, so you need some help. If you don't mind me asking, what are you noticing about yourself that is telling you that you need some help?
>
> **Jessica:** I'm not eating enough. Oh, my gosh, I can't believe I said that! [pauses] Like, I pretty much eat an orange for breakfast, and a yogurt for lunch. I can't believe I'm telling you this!
>
> **SSW:** Wow, okay. So, you feel like you're really not eating enough.
>
> **Jessica:** No, I'm not. And the other part is . . . Well, I really don't know if I can tell you the other part.
>
> **SSW:** Okay.
>
> **Jessica:** Well, I work out a lot. Like, a LOT, like, way more than my friends. I wake up at five and go to the gym for an hour, then I go to school, then I go to practice, then I work out at home for another hour before bed.

SSW: Okay, yes, that does sound like a lot. I bet that's exhausting!

Jessica: [nodding] It is.

In this section, the school social worker asks questions such as "How are you hoping that I can be helpful to you?" and "What are you noticing about yourself that is telling you that you need some help?" to begin to elicit the student's understanding of the problem and what she would like to be different. During this beginning stage in SFBT, we listen respectfully to the "problem-talk," or the client's description of the problem from her own perspective. We then guide the conversation toward "solution-talk," where we begin to think about and describe what will be different for the client when her problems are solved (De Jong & Berg, 2008).

Section 3: Beginning to Generate Solution-Talk

SSW: Can I ask you a question that you may need to think about for a minute?

Jessica: Okay.

SSW: Suppose we have a great conversation today, and it's really helpful to you. So helpful, in fact, that it really gets you going on making some changes. Then let's say maybe even later today, tomorrow, the next day, or even later this week, you start to notice these changes. What will be different about you that will show you that talking with me today really helped?

Jessica: Wow, that's a hard question. [silence] Well, the problem is that I want to change, I know I need to eat more and work out less, but I also don't wanna change. I kind of feel better when I'm doing things this way, you know? Even though I know it's wrong.

SSW: Hmm, so part of you wants to change, and part of you doesn't. I'm just curious, you know, about that part of you that wants to change. Can I just ask you about that part for a minute?

Jessica: Mmm-hmm.

SSW: So, that part of you that wants to change, what is telling that part of you that change is important right now for you?

Jessica: That part of me knows that what I'm doing is unhealthy, and it wants me to eat more and rest more and not spend all my time working out. And it thinks that, I don't know, that those changes are just, like, the right thing to do.

SSW: Wow, that part of you sounds really wise. The right thing to do, huh? What tells you that eating more and resting more and not working out so much are the right thing to do?

Jessica: Well, that's what normal people do. And what my parents would want me to do, and Tia.

SSW: Oh, yeah, the people you care about. So, they would be happy if you made some changes?

Jessica: Well, Tia definitely would. I'm not sure about my parents because I think I've been hiding things from them pretty well.

In Section 3, the school social worker begins to generate solution-talk by asking questions like "What will be different about you that will show you that talking with me today really helped?" and "What is telling that part of you that change is important right now for you?" These questions are generally useful because they give the student the opportunity to begin constructing a preferred future, where the problems that she is struggling with have been solved. In this section, you can observe the student's ambivalence about change, which is often present in students with eating disorders. The school social worker listens to her, affirms her experience, and also chooses to ask her questions about the part of her that wants to change.

Section 4: Continuing Solution-Talk and Beginning to Develop Goals

SSW: Okay. Let's say that you and I work together, and we become a really great team, and we really get you making some changes in your life. And then we turn out to be really successful, so successful that you don't even need to come back and see me anymore because you're doing great. When that happens, what will we notice about you that will really show us that you're doing better?

Jessica: Well . . . I would be happier. Yeah, I'd be a lot happier, and a lot calmer. And I would be feeling good about myself. [pauses] You know, I think maybe I'd love myself instead of hating myself.

SSW: Wow, those sound like a lot of good changes. So let's see, you'd be happier, calmer, feeling good about yourself, and loving yourself . . . Anything else?

Jessica: Yeah, I wouldn't care what the other girls said about me. And I wouldn't worry so much about my grades, or about if a boy will ever like me. Or about college.

SSW: So a lot fewer worries. And, um, what will we see you doing instead of worrying?

Jessica: Well, I guess enjoying things. And . . . I probably wouldn't have so many problems with the eating and working out stuff.

SSW: Oh, really, wow, what do you think you'll notice about yourself that will show you that you're having less problems with that stuff?

Jessica: Well, I'll just do it more like I did before. You know, like a regular breakfast, a regular lunch, things that normal people do. And probably just working out at practice and nothing else. But that'd be really hard for me!

SSW: Yeah. Yeah. So . . . oh, I don't want to miss this, you said "like I did before"—does that mean that you used to have less problems with eating and working out?

Jessica: Yeah, I would say, like, freshman year I was pretty normal, you know. I ate regular amounts and was just like a regular high school girl athlete. I guess that was before I got so worried, and then it just started feeling like doing all that stuff was helping or something. I don't know. It's weird.

In this section, the school social worker is asking the student questions to focus her mind on further defining her preferred future when she is doing well. The questions she asks and her follow-up responses invite the student to give further details about her preferred future. Through this process, the school social worker and the student are able to begin defining some of the goals that are important to the student—feeling happier, feeling calmer, feeling good about herself, and so forth. At the end of the section, the school social worker also asks an exception question and discovers that there was a time when the student was doing better. Exception questions are useful because they can "help clients become more aware of their current and past successes in relation to their goals" (De Jong & Berg, 2008, p. 105).

Section 5: Amplifying what the Student Wants and Further Developing Goals

SSW: Yeah, okay. So that's when things changed. You know, can I ask you a strange question?

Jessica: Okay.

SSW: Let's say you leave my office today and you go about the rest of your day like normal. You finish your classes, you go to practice, you go home, you have dinner, you go to sleep at your normal time, and you happen to fall into a really deep sleep. And while you're sleeping, a miracle happens. And the miracle is that the problems that brought you here have been solved, so you're happier, calmer, feeling good about yourself, all those things are better. But the tricky thing is, the miracle happened while you were asleep, so when you first wake up, you don't know that it happened. So, when you wake up tomorrow and this miracle has happened, what's the first small thing you notice that lets you know your miracle has happened?

Jessica: [thinking] Well, I wouldn't wake up so early.

SSW: [encouraging] Okay.

Jessica: Yeah, I would wake up at six with my alarm instead of at five, because my mind would be better, more calm, so I would stay asleep.

SSW: Wow, so the first thing that will really show you that your miracle has happened will be when you wake up at six with a more calm mind.

Jessica: Yeah, my mind will be more calm, and actually waking up at six would be a really big change because, then, well, if it's really a miracle, I won't have worked out in the morning before I go to school.

SSW: Yeah, you're right. So, after your miracle has happened, you'll wake up at six, your mind will be calmer, and you won't be working out before school. What will you be doing instead?

Jessica: Well, probably just getting ready.

SSW: Yeah, and how will that go differently now that your miracle has happened?

Jessica: Well, I would feel more calm, so I'd be thinking ahead that maybe it would be a good day at school. And I'd be less tired because I slept longer, so I would probably not be so slow getting ready, so I could really sit down at the table for breakfast.

SSW: Wow, yeah. And so we'll see you sitting down at the table for breakfast. And how will that change things?

Jessica: Well, it's a miracle, so I will eat a healthy breakfast.

SSW: Oh, yeah, like what will we see you eating?

Jessica: Probably oatmeal with fruit and nuts. That's what I used to eat.

SSW: Great, so we'll see you eating oatmeal with fruit and nuts at the table. How will that make your day go better?

Jessica: Well, since it's a miracle, it won't make me feel fat.

SSW: Yeah, definitely, and how will that change things for you?

Jessica: Well, I won't have to spend all morning thinking about how fat I look because I ate that for breakfast.

SSW: Yeah, what will you be doing instead all morning?

Jessica: Well, really paying attention to things more at school. Like I already pay attention, but it takes so much work because there is this whole other thing going on in my brain about what I ate and being fat and what I will eat and what I look like to other people and stuff. So since that will be gone, I'll really just sort of pay attention and maybe even enjoy my classes, at least the ones I like.

SSW: Wow, so you'll really be able to just pay attention and enjoy them.

Jessica: Yeah, and I'll have more energy, too, because I won't have woken up so early, and I won't be so tired from working out and not eating almost anything. It's really hard! [tears up]

SSW: Yeah. That sounds hard. [pauses] So, you'll have more energy?

Jessica: [smiling a little] Yeah.

SSW: How will that make your day go better?

Jessica: Oh, a lot better. I'll want to talk to my friends at lunch, and then I guess since it's a miracle I'll eat more of a lunch, and then I'll maybe have some pep in my step in the afternoon.

SSW: Great, more pep in your step. And what will you be doing differently once you have more pep in your step?

Jessica: Well, I'll just be handling everything more easily, so if a teacher gives an assignment I'll be like "I can do that" instead of just starting to worry that I won't do it perfectly.

SSW: Oooh, I love that, you'll be like "I can do that".

Jessica: Yeah, and I'll be feeling more good about myself, like I said before, loving myself. [tears up] That would be really different for me.

SSW: Yeah, that sounds important to you. How will things be different for you when you are feeling good about yourself and loving yourself?

Jessica: [silent for a bit] I'll just, you know, feel better inside. I won't want to do things to punish myself, like not eating.

SSW: What will you want to be doing instead of punishing yourself when you're feeling good about yourself?

Jessica: I guess being nice to myself, telling myself I'm doing a good job, rewarding myself, like maybe by doing something fun.

SSW: That sounds great.

Jessica: Yeah.

SSW: And after your miracle happens tonight, who do you think will be the first person to notice the change in you?

Jessica: Oh, definitely Tia.

SSW: Oh, yeah? What will she notice about you that will show her that your miracle has happened?

Jessica: [tears in her eyes] I'll seem happy.

SSW: That's great. What will Tia notice about you that will really show her that you're happy?

Jessica: I'll be smiling. I'll have pep in my step. I'll be saying good things about myself. And I'll be eating my lunch and

not saying I'm fat, and just, like . . . back to myself before.
Like, how I used to be.

SSW: Back to yourself.

Jessica: Yeah.

The miracle question is one of the most important techniques in SFBT to further develop student goals and amplify what the student wants. As described by De Jong and Berg (2008), "the miracle question requests clients to make a leap of faith and imagine how their life will be changed when the problem is solved" (p. 84). They further explain that this is particularly useful because "it gives clients permission to think about an unlimited range of possibilities" (p. 84) and "begins to move the focus away from their current and past problems and toward a more satisfying life" (p. 84).

In this section, the school social worker asked the initial miracle question, and then asked a number of follow-up questions that encourage the student to create a more detailed picture of her miracle. During this process, the school social worker and student are able to uncover a lot more information about what the student would like to be different and how those differences will be helpful to her. The school social worker asks questions such as "How will that go differently?" and "How will that change things?" to give the student the opportunity to elaborate more fully on how the desired changes will positively impact her life. The school social worker also asks the student the question "What will you be doing instead?" multiple times, to give her the chance to consider what positive things will be in her life in place of the things she is trying to move away from. In addition, the school social worker asks for details about who would notice the change in the student, and what that person would notice, to help the student begin to imagine her changes in interactional terms. All of this detail helps to create a more vivid picture of what the student wants to be moving toward, and helps her goals to become more concrete, behavioral, and measurable. For example, instead of just stopping at the more vague goal of "having more energy," the school social worker and the student are able to define that when she has more energy, Jessica will want to talk to her friends at lunch, eat her lunch, have pep in her step in the afternoon, find it easier to handle things in class, and if a teacher gives her an assignment, she will feel like she can handle it.

SSW: Jessica, would it be okay for me to draw you a small picture?

Jessica: Sure.

SSW: [draws a scale on a piece of paper] Let's say this is a scale from 0 to 10, with 10 being your total miracle happening all the time and 0 being the total opposite of your miracle happening all the time. Does that make sense?

Jessica: Yeah.

SSW: So, on this scale then, where would you say you are these days?

Jessica: [pointing on the scale] Probably like a 2.

SSW: Okay, thanks. [draws the 2] And, um, what lets you know you're at the 2 instead of something lower, like a 0?

Jessica: What? Oh ... Well, I'm still getting good grades.

SSW: Yes, you are. What else?

Jessica: I do eat some. And sometimes I feel okay about myself.

SSW: Great. What else?

Jessica: I have friends.

SSW: Yeah! What else?

Jessica: I think that's all.

SSW: Okay, great. So, let me ask you, in terms of our work together, what number will you be satisfied with in the end?

Jessica: Like, you and me working together? What number when we're done?

SSW: Exactly.

Jessica: [thinking] Well, I wanna be at a 10. But that sounds so far off. Maybe a 7?

SSW: Sounds good. Let me draw that for you. [draws the 7] So, what are the biggest things that you'll notice about yourself that will really show you that you're at a 7?

Jessica: I'm happy. And calmer. And like I said, feeling good about myself. Maybe even starting to love myself a little bit. And you know, eating better and working out less. And also talking to my friends more. And paying attention better in class.

SSW: That's a lot of great stuff! Like you'll be back to yourself?
Jessica: Yeah.

In this section, the school social worker utilizes scaling questions with the student to begin to define where the student is and where she wants to go within the frame of reference of her miracle. As described by De Jong and Berg (2008), "scaling is a useful technique for making complex aspects of the client's life more concrete and accessible to both practitioner and client" (p. 107). In this case, scaling the miracle is a useful process because it brings the miracle back into reality and allows the student to identify the bits of her miracle that are already happening. In addition, it helps the student to consider how close she perceives that she will need to be to her miracle picture in order to be satisfied, and also what changes will be the most important to her success. This emphasizes to the student that she does not need to make her miracle picture happen in its entirety to consider herself successful—she only has to get to a better place, as defined by herself. Asking about the point on the miracle scale where the student will be satisfied also gives the school social worker and the student an opportunity in the first session to imagine the endpoint of therapy. This helps to emphasize the brief nature of SFBT—it assumes that the student will not be in therapy forever and, in fact, will stop working with the school social worker when she is ready to continue the change process on her own.

Section 7: Break, Feedback, and Task Setting

SSW: Excellent. So, usually toward the end of a visit, I like to take a break for about two or three minutes. I actually leave the room and think about everything we talked about today, and then I come back and give you some things to think about until I see you again. Would it be okay with you for me to do that now?
Jessica: Okay.
SSW: Before I take my break, I always like to ask, is there anything that you didn't get to say today that you still wanted to say?
Jessica: No, I actually said a lot more than I thought I would.
SSW: Okay, then I will see you in just a few minutes.
[The SSW leaves and then returns.]

SSW: All right, here is what really stands out for me today. I first just really wanted to compliment you for coming in here today to talk with me about this stuff. I know it's not easy to talk about, so I've really been saying to myself, what a brave young woman! I'm also impressed with the wise part of you that is interested in making some changes, and that you were able to really spell out those changes so well for me today. In particular, I loved what you said about feeling calm and happy, loving yourself, eating and working out in ways that are healthier, which shows that you are back to yourself. And I thought it was neat to see that you are already at a 2 on your miracle scale, so we are not starting from a 0. So, I wanted to give you a little task to do between now and next time we meet, if that would be okay with you?

Jessica: Okay.

SSW: Can you please pay really good attention so that you notice any times when you are at the 2 or even a little bit higher sometimes?

Jessica: Like, notice when I'm doing a little better?

SSW: Yes. And really notice what is different that shows you that you're doing a little bit better. Maybe you're thinking a little better, feeling a little better, doing something a little bit better.

Jessica: Okay, I think I can do that.

SSW: Great, you can even jot some of them down to help you remember for next time if you want to.

Jessica: Okay.

SSW: Do you have any questions about anything we talked about today?

Jessica: No.

SSW: Great. And my very last question, I promise, is what was the most helpful to you today, from everything that we talked about?

Jessica: [pauses] My miracle. Because it's nice to think that something like that might be able to happen to me.

SSW: Definitely.

In Section 7, the school social worker utilizes a break so that she can reflect on the session and formulate feedback that will hopefully be helpful to the student. During this break, the school social worker considers what the student has said that she wants to have different, the things that social worker is genuinely impressed with about the student that relate to what the student wants to have different, and what the social worker thinks could be a useful task for the student to complete between sessions. The school social worker then returns, delivers the compliments, and follows with the task request. In this case, the school social worker chooses the task of noticing times when the student is doing a little bit better in an attempt to draw the student's attention to these times for multiple reasons. First, this will allow the student to observe and experience herself doing better, which will build her confidence in her ability to continue changing. Second, the student will be able to make observations about what she is doing differently when she is doing better, which will give her good clues about which behaviors, thoughts, and feelings she would like to replicate. Lastly, simply by paying attention to the times when she is doing better, the student may end up having more times when she is doing better because her mind will be dwelling in this reality more of the time.

At the very end of the session, the school social worker asks what was most helpful to the student that day. This is useful because the student's reply may give the social worker some clues about what can be done in future sessions that will be most useful to the student. It is also a nice way to conclude the conversation because it leaves the student with something positive to take away from the session.

References

Alegria, M., Woo, M., Cao, Z., Torres, M., Meng, X., & Striegel-Moore, R. (2007). Prevalence and correlates of eating disorders in Latinos in the United States. *International Journal of Eating Disorders, 40,* S15–S21. doi: 10.1002/eat.20406

American Psychiatric Association. (2013). *Diagnostic and statistical manual of mental disorders (5th ed.).* Arlington, VA: American Psychiatric Publishing.

De Jong, P., & Berg, I. K. (2008). *Interviewing for solutions* (3rd ed.). Belmont, CA: Brooks/Cole.

Frank, G. K. W. (2015). What causes eating disorders, and what do they cause? *Biological Psychiatry, 77,* 602–603.

Heller, N. R., & Lu, J. (2015). Eating disorders and treatment planning. In K. Corcoran & A. R. Roberts (Eds.), *Social workers' desk reference* (3rd ed., pp. 571–578). New York, NY: Oxford University Press.

Jacobi, C., Fittig, E., Bryson, S. W., Wilfley, D., Kraemer, H. C., & Taylor, C. B. (2011). Who is really at risk? Identifying risk factors for subthreshold and full syndrome eating disorders in a high-risk sample. *Psychological Medicine, 41*, 1939–1949. doi: 10.1017/S0033291710002631

Keel, P. K., & Forney, K. J. (2013). Psychosocial risk factors for eating disorders. *International Journal of Eating Disorders, 46*, 433–439.

Kelly, M. S., Thompson, A. M., Frey, A., Klemp, H., Alvarez, M., & Berzin, S. C. (2015). The state of school social work: Revisited. *School Mental Health, 7*(3), 174–183.

Martin, C. V., Guterman, J. T., & Shatz, K. (2012). Solution-focused counseling for eating disorders. Retrieved from: http://www.counseling.org/resources/library/vistas/2012_vol_1_67-104/2_2012-aca-pdfs/article_88.pdf

Pomeroy, E. C., & Browning, P. Y. (2013). Eating disorders. *Encyclopedia of Social Work*. doi:10.1093/acrefore/9780199975839.013.117

Shuttlesworth, M., & Zotter, D. (2009). Disordered eating in African American and Caucasian women: The role of ethnic identity. *Journal of Black Studies, 42*, 906–922.

Smink, F. R. E., van Hoeken, D., & Hoek, H. W. (2012). Epidemiology of eating disorders: Incidence, prevalence, and mortality rates. *Current Psychiatry Reports, 14*, 406–414. doi:10.1007/s11920-012-0282-y

Stice, E., Marti, C. N., & Durant, S. (2011). Risk factors for onset of eating disorders: Evidence of multiple risk pathways from an 8-year prospective study. *Behavior Research and Therapy, 49*, 622–627. doi:10.1016/j.brat.2011.06.009

Trace, S. E., Baker, J. H., Penas-Lledo, E., & Bulik, C. M. (2013). The genetics of eating disorders. *Annual Review of Clinical Psychology, 9*, 589–620. doi:10.1146/annurev-clinpsy-050212-185546.

Zalta, A. K., & Keel, P. K. (2006). Peer influence on bulimic symptoms in college students. *Journal of Abnormal Psychology, 115*, 185–189.

Index

abstinence
  defined, 153, 154
  secondary, 154
abuse. *See* child abuse and neglect
academic problems, 34–36*t*
acknowledging student's
    feelings, 141
affirmative relationships with
    students, keys to, 111
aggression, 60–61
Akos, P., 129
anorexia nervosa (AN), 179–80
  diagnostic criteria, 179
  subtypes, 180
anxiety, solutions to, 96, 98
  eight-week SFBT group for
    student anxiety, 96,
    97–98*b*, 98
approach goals, 132
at-risk students. *See also* risk factors
  solution-based approach for, 57–61
avoid goals, 131

Baldwin, Victoria, 56
Bannink, F., 124
behavior problems, 34–36*t*
Berg, Insoo Kim, 13–14, 74, 77, 79,
    111–13, 121, 132, 138, 140,
    141, 144, 191, 193

binge eating, 180
binge-eating disorder (BED), 180
  diagnostic criteria, 180–81
body image and eating
    disorders, 181
bridging statements, providing, 147
Brief Family Therapy Center
    (BFTC), 32
Britain. *See* United Kingdom
broaden-and-build theory of
    positive emotions, 14–15
Browning, P. Y., 182
bulimia nervosa (BN), 180
  diagnostic criteria, 180

case study process, a
    solution-focused, 88–89
change
  defining what the student wants
    to have different, 184–85
  SFBT theory of, 13–15
change party, 104
child abuse and neglect, 124–25.
    See also mandated reporting
  abuse and trauma in
    schools, 107–8
  child maltreatment in United
    States, 108–9
  trust and safety

child abuse and neglect (*Cont.*)
  factors helpful in building a
    sense of, 111–12
  importance in recovery and
    thriving, 110–12
cognitive-behavioral therapy (CBT),
  4, 131–32
  CBT social worker model, 14*b*
  contrasted with SFBT, 13, 14*b*,
    17, 21, 131–32
Communities in Schools (CIS), 59
community schools, 90
compliments of client by
  clinician, 21
congruence. *See* incongruence
coping dialogue, engaging student
  in a, 138–41
coping questions, 21–23, 138, 141
cultural competence, gaining, 9

Darmody, M., 133
De Jong, Peter, 31, 138, 140, 141,
  144, 191, 193
de Shazer, Steve, 13–14
doing something different, 23
Dolan, Y., 136
Durant, S., 181

eating disorders
  case example, 183–95
  causes, 181–82
  definitions and
    descriptions, 179–81
  reasons for using SFBT
    approach, 182–83
Eggert, L. L., 130–31
Eisengart, S., 32–33
elders. *See* GRGs

emotions. *See also* feelings
  negative, 15
  positive, 14–15
Erford, B. T., 128
European Brief Therapy
  Association, 47
exception questions, 17–18
expectations, 19
experimentation, defined, 154

family therapy, SFBT, 90–94
feedback, providing, 176, 193–95
feelings. *See also* emotions
  acknowledging, validating,
    and normalizing
    student's, 141–43
Fiske, H., 133, 139
follow-up questions, 145
Frank, G. K. W., 181
Fredrickson, B., 14–15
future description,
  preferred, 166–76

Galassi, J. P., 129
Garner, J., 25, 27
Garza High School, 52–53, 71.
  See also Tier 1 framework
  academic achievement and
    success, 65–69
  data collected by school
    district, 69–70
  implementing SFBT in the alter-
    native school, 61–63
  as model program, 70–71
  schoolwide examples of SFBT
    principles, 63, 64*b*, 65
  solution-based approach for
    at-risk students, 57–61

training philosophy, 54–55
ways teachers used solution-
    building intervention
    skills, 57
goal formation process
    amplifying what the student
        wants, 188–91
    assisting student with, 143–44
    beginning to develop
        goals, 186–88
    students not ready to
        start, 138–41
goal setting, 20–21. *See also* task
    setting
grandparents raising grandchildren.
    See GRGs
GRG ideas, orientation to, 99
GRG parenting problems, iden-
    tifying exceptions to
    presenting, 102–3
GRGs (grandparents raising
    grandchildren)
    identifying strengths as a
        grandparent and applying
        them to your mission as a
        GRG, 99–100
    a solution-focused parent group
        for, 88, 98–104
    using SFBT interventions in daily
        life with grandchildren, 103
    ways to keep going as a
        GRG, 103
GRG wisdom night, 104
groups, SFBT, 96, 97–98*b*, 98

Henden, J., 133, 134, 136,
    139–44, 146–48
hope-building process, 148

incongruence, assessing for, 137
individualized education plans
    (IEPs), 9–10

Kelly, Michael, 74–75
Kelly, S., 113, 121

language, client
    picking up the, 162–66
Lévi-Strauss, Claude, 148
life lessons, panel of elders
    sharing, 104

Madden, B., 133
mandated reporting
    being a mandated
        reporter, 112–13
    and beyond, 114–24
Marti, C. N., 181
mental health issues. *See also*
    specific issues
    prevalence, 126–28
    student risk and protective
        factors, 128–31
mental health services,
    school-based, 5–6
meta-analysis, 33, 37*b*, 37–39, 39*t*
    definition and overview, 37*b*
Metcalf, L., 144
microsuccesses, 138
Miller, S. D., 31
miracle question, 166, 191
miracle scale, 192–93
Mix-It-Up Days, 63
motivational interviewing
    (MI), 16–17
moving forward, questions related
    to, 18*b*

Multi-tiered System of Supports/
Response to Intervention
framework, 87. *See also*
Response to Intervention
(RtI) framework; three-tier
system; Tier 1 framework;
Tier 3 framework; WOWW
program
Murphy, J. J., 145–46

needs assessment,
solution-focused, 94–95
neuroception, 109
neuroscience and solution-
focused engagement with
students, 109–10
Newsome, D. W., 128
Newsome, S., 97–98

O'Connell, M. E., 130
Olson, K., 109

parent group, solution-focused,
88, 98–104
Patterson, L. E., 129
Peterson, C., 99–100
Pomeroy, E. C., 182
Porges, Stephen, 109
positive emotions theory, 14–15
positive psychology, 14
pre-session change, 17
problem-free talk
purposes, 134
used at beginning of
session, 133–34
problem-solving discussions, 17
problem-talk, avoiding, 175–76

protective factors, 155–56. *See also
under* mental health issues
defined, 130
psychotherapy, history of, 12–13
Public Health Service Act, 128–29

questions (to ask student in SFBT),
17–18, 18*b*. *See also* miracle
question
to elicit suicidal ideation if
present, 137–38
follow-up, 145
"Why," 142

Rak, C. F., 129
rapport, developing rapid, 133–34
Ratner, H., 114
recovery, defined, 154
resiliency, 128–30
defined, 129
resistance, 23–24
Response to Intervention (RtI)
framework, 52, 53. *See
also* Multi-tiered System
of Supports/Response to
Intervention framework
risk factors, 128–31, 155–56, 156*t*
Rock, E., 128
Rogers, Carl R., 113

safety. *See under* child abuse and
neglect
Saleebey, D., 31
scaling, 193
school readiness factors, 61
schools
community, 90

solution-building
  characteristics of, 27*b*
  planning exercise for
    developing, 27*b*
solutions (to problems) in, 3–4
steps for determining readiness
  and helping them move
  toward use of SFBT, 61–62
school social worker (SSW). *See also*
  specific topics
  task of, 16
school staff
  interprofessional training on
    SFBT, 54–57*t*
  ways to improve competencies
    of, 62–63
self-harm, 58, 59*b*
Seligman, Martin E. P., 99
sexual abuse, 114–18. *See also* child
  abuse and neglect
SFBT (solution-focused brief therapy), 1. *See also specific topics*
  advantages in a school
    setting, 6, 6*b*
  SFBT as client centered, 7
  SFBT as strengths based, 6–7
  SFBT can be adapted to special
    education IEP goals, 9–10
  SFBT can be as brief (or long)
    as you want, 8–9
  SFBT enables practitioners to
    gain cultural competence, 9
  SFBT is adaptable, 8
  SFBT is portable, 8
  SFBT makes small changes
    matter, 7–8
  application, 25

contrasted with other counseling
  approaches, 131–32. *See also*
  cognitive-behavioral therapy
contrasted with other strengths-
  based interventions, 16
future of, 28, 104–5
historical background, 12–13
how it distinguishes itself, 16–17
overview, 28
reasons it is suited to school
  social work practice, 4–6
steps for determining school's
  readiness and helping school
  move toward use of, 61–62
what it does and does not
  teach, 24–25
SFBT research, 25, 27–28, 31–32
early research studies, 32
implications for practice in
  schools, 45–47
meta-analyses, 33, 37*b*,
  37–39, 39*t*
in school settings, 40, 41–44*t*
systematic reviews,
  32–33, 34–36*t*
SFBT session(s)
establishing the desired outcome
  of the talk, 159–62
first session. *See* eating disorders: case example
goal setting and future, 20–21
taking a break during, 193–95
using problem-free talk at beginning of, 133–34
wrapping up the, 148
SFBT skills, 15–16
SFBT studies. *See* SFBT research

SFBT techniques, 17–20.
  See also specific techniques
Sharry, J., 133, 136–37, 144
Shilts, Lee, 74, 77, 79
Shilts, Margaret, 77
social worker models of SFBT and
  CBT, 14*b*. *See also*
  cognitive-behavioral
  therapy
solution building, 16
solution-focused brief therapy.
  See SFBT
Solution-Focused Brief
  Therapy Association
  (SFBTA), 15, 47
solution-focused school, starting
  your own, 70–71
*Solution Focused Therapy Treatment
  Manual for Working with
  Individuals*, 16
solutions, looking for, 18*b*
solution-talk
  beginning to generate, 185–86
  continuing, 186–88
Star Walk, 63, 64*b*
Steiner, T., 111–12, 121
Stice, E., 181
Streeter, C. L., 25, 26, 55
students. *See also specific topics*
  how to view, 113
substance abuse
  case example, 157–77
  definitions, 153–54
  overview of SFBT
    approach, 157–58
  overview of substance abuse
    nationally in schools, 153

prevalence rates among school-aged
  persons, 154–55
  adolescent substance use
    percentages, 154, 155*t*
  protective factors, 155–56
  research about SFBT with, 156
  risk factors, 155–56, 156*t*
  symptom indicators, 154
substance dependence, defined, 154
substance use. *See also*
  substance abuse
  defined, 153
success, measuring your, 26*b*
suicidal ideation
  identification of, 132–33
  acknowledging, validating,
    and normalizing student's
    feelings, 141–43
  asking for a brief description of
    student's concern, 135–37
  assessing for
    incongruence, 137
  assisting the student in identi-
    fying exceptions, 145–46
  case study, 132–48
  complimenting the
    student, 146–47
  developing rapid rapport
    by using "problem-free
    talk" at beginning of
    session, 133–34
  encouraging student to go slow
    and take small steps, 144
  engaging student in a coping
    dialogue, 138–41
  wrapping up the session, 148
  normalizing, 142–43

questions designed to
elicit, 137–38
suicide risk (SR), 58, 59*b*, 130–31

tasks, identifying, 147
task setting, 193–95. *See also* goal
setting
teachers
are people too, 76–77
ways of using solution-building
intervention skills, 57
ways to improve competencies
of, 62–63
teachers lounge, looking for solutions in, 74–76
therapist characteristics and
requirements, 47*b*
three-tier system, 53. *See also* Multi-
tiered System of Supports/
Response to Intervention
framework; Tier 1 frame-
work; Tier 3 framework;
WOWW program
Tier 1 framework, 53–54, 71–72.
See also Garza High School
designing a solution-focused
school using, 54–57
Tier 2 framework. *See* WOWW
program
Tier 3 framework, case studies
of, 88–104

transdisciplinary approach to
solving problems, 55
trauma. *See* child abuse and
neglect
trust. *See under* child abuse and
neglect

United Kingdom (UK), WOWW
in, 83–84

validating student's
feelings, 141–42
Values in Action (VIA)
questionnaire, 100
violence, 60–61

Walsh, E., 130–31
Watson, Sam, 61
Webb, Linda, 56, 70, 71
"Why" questions, 142
WOWW coaching, goals of, 78
WOWW coaching process, phases
for, 79*b*
WOWW program (Working on
What Works), 74–77
future of, 84–85
history of, 77
research on, 82–84
skills used in, 77–78, 80–82

Yusuf, D., 114